AF787474

MASQUERADE AT THE CROSSROADS OF GOOD AND EVIL

MASQUERADE AT THE CROSSROADS OF GOOD AND EVIL

Holism and Spirit Work in Mental Health and Addiction

David Stokes

AEON

First published in 2026 by
Aeon Books

British Library Cataloguing in Publication Data

A C.I.P. for this book is available from the British Library

ISBN-13: 978-1-80152-215-1

Typeset by Medlar Publishing Solutions Pvt Ltd, India

www.aeonbooks.co.uk

CONTENTS

To begin

Every age has a corresponding set of tastes, a codex of what's possible and within acceptable limits to say, and what's not to say. Our present age is no different. Within the many hierarchies and parts that make up society, there are things that can be said and listened to, and things that can be said but will not be listened to. In our times in the field of mental health the pharmaceutical industry for the most part shapes what is promoted and listened to, by virtue of its funding and research likes and dislikes. Although there are movements opposed to both the psychiatric and pharmaceutical last word on almost everything, they have yet to make an any real impact on so many of the actual events that happen daily in the lives of those diagnosed with serious mental health conditions.

After many years supporting the mentally ill and addicted in both what is euphemistically referred to as "the community", and in residential settings that were often the successors to the old asylums, I found out the hard way that the following points are critical in holistic spirit work in this field. Firstly, a gestalt approach is necessary. Everything must be well thought through and reflected on: economic status, sexuality, history of trauma, family dynamics and familial roles, the specific nature of each presenting mental health manifestation of dysfunction, environment, and most importantly the personalities in the immediate healing space. We must remember that, consciously as well as otherwise, not everyone wishes the best for others, even if they happen to be psychiatrists, mental health workers or managers, medical staff, fellow patients, and family members. Motivations are grounded in personal psychology, family dynamics that can reach back to previous generations, practical matters involving money, and status. All that can be quite an obstacle to helping someone move on in a therapeutic and psychic sense.

Secondly, the malaise is often so entrenched that trust must be formed before anything positive can be done. The dysfunctional thinking at the root of serious psychiatric and addictive self-destructiveness is so enmeshed with the individual's own thought-life that to try to remove such thinking could be seen as an attempt to remove a person's entire thought-life and personality, a kind of benign method of therapeutic annihilation of the personality. Thirdly, and most importantly, the helper must keep an open mind. I've never personally met a psychiatrist who came across as actually believing the "mental illness is caused by chemical imbalance in the brain" line from psychopharmacology's golden rules handbook. Who would believe such a thing, especially having spent long periods of time among those with enduring mental health diagnoses? We have a duty to ask the questions that are not expedient for us to ask but must be asked. Questions such as:

> What if the voices experienced in schizophrenia are not hallucinations? What if they are real?

Among so many vested interests, it's a quite a challenge to bring ideas from history and other realms of study into the fields of mental health recovery. Even after much reflection and time they still emanate truth. We are obliged to find new ways of saying today what was said in the past. Are the disturbing voices so often found in schizophrenia in keeping with the Emanuel Swedenborg tradition crystallized in the work of experimentalists like Dr. Wilson Van Dusen? Looked at from outside the lens of the pharmaceutical hierarchy, it is plausible that the voices experienced in schizophrenia are not hallucinations, but rather invisible parasites not part of the material world. There are surely other ways to phrase this in a civilization where psychopharmacology is pretty much in control and is grounded in a materialist view of the cosmos which has become less convincing.

A natural conduit between Swedenborg's time and today's age of reason—or some might say age of cynicism—is the work of Carl Jung. Is it more acceptable to suggest that the voices and personalities experienced by those suffering paranoid schizophrenia are mutated archetypes, as much as we understand such things from readings of Jung's most lucid work? Jung's scholarship and recognition in the annals of psychology make this method of interpretation more palatable in an age yet dominated by the reductive philosophy of a particular view of science guided by neo-Darwinians.

With matters as they stand, and in the time-frame in which we live, a masquerade is necessary, because to make a true and honest attempt at addressing the suffering involved in mental health dysfunction, we need to go deep into the psyche and yet deeper into the spiritual truths underpinning our very existence. Where necessary we must masquerade as drones in thrall to the psychopharmacological dogma, to the biological imperative that centres all dysfunction in brain science. Then with the appropriate flags of acquiescence raised high in the air we can do what spirit work it's possible to do at a crossroads filled with both darkness and light, good and evil.

Frank

It's a moment of déjà vu. A mental health worker is fidgeting with her pen. A resident in a mental health care-home looks restlessly at a wall-clock on the other side of the room as if wishing he was anywhere but here. A state psychiatrist gives every impression of going through the motions, taking on the part much like an actor slipping into character. Has he bothered to rehearse his lines? There's a sense of phoniness to the whole business, a tacit agreement between all parties to act out their agreed roles as convincingly as they can. We have been here before. The faces are different, but the scenario is pretty much unchanged. For those working or volunteering in mental health, or drawn into the world of state-administered psychiatric intervention through a family member, loved one, or friend, it would be all too familiar.

The care-home manager is running late and apologises a little breathlessly to the psychiatrist as she enters the room and takes her place at the table. She is into the talking therapy side of things, has a counselling qualification, and is quick to see anything remotely positive or innovative, anything at all that might signify a tiny shift in someone's condition. Not much is going on after all. Nobody around here is making much headway. The psychiatrist's eyes are closing. It's mid-afternoon and perhaps he's lunched well. He shows a confident, benign face to the world, often referred to in the hierarchy he is part of as "being professional". The mental health worker is now reading notes relating to the outpatient we are here to talk about today. Is the psychiatrist even listening? There's a spiritlessness in the functional room, just like the spiritlessness that's so often in such places. Everything here speaks of state-sector institutionalism.

A number of experts and authorial voices are tuned into the probable causal factors of such spiritlessness but maybe it has just got to do with our fundamental human condition. Have we less need for connections with spirit in a technocratic age where it can seem as if we're lost to ourselves, strangers to our inner selves as much as to each other? There is no time for a line from Thoth's prophecy or the Sermon on the Mount or from any of the pithy sayings of Thich Nhat Hanh. It's a secular affair with a psychic amnesia hanging like a low dark cloud over everything. There is nothing on the walls to remind us that we are part of a culture, no dated and somewhat gaudy portrait of a monarch or framed quote of a war-time leader. No Hippocratic oath or line or two from the Serenity Prayer. All that's missing to put the finishing touches to the dystopian mood is a whiff of cabbage water and bleach. We could be literally anywhere, meeting up to discuss anything. What could shift any of this from the trough it has settled in? A quest to find out just what's going on is a beginning, a first step on a long road that weaves in and out of innumerable pitfalls. The matter in hand after all is human suffering.

In these emotionally sterile rooms there's always a sense that everyone present is walking on eggshells, afraid of offending someone or other who isn't actually present, at least not in a physical sense. With an increased population and changing demographics it is easier to get lost in moral equivalence, easier to sidestep moral templates by defaulting to a kind of moral relativism. The good is obscured behind a myriad of complexities to do with the cult of the personality and a new creed that gives everyone legally protected rights but often places on their shoulders a weight of individual responsibility that fewer than we think can bear for very long.

Not everyone can walk in the world without some kind of supportive community that is real rather than just written down somewhere in a risk assessment. The social and spiritual alienation of so many in developed countries, where consumerist culture and veneration of technology has mutated out of recognition to any intended model, is pitiful to see. Warnings of spiritual nihilism have been around for some time. In *Choruses from the Rock* TS Eliot speaks to us from 1934:

> Endless invention, endless experiments, Brings knowledge of motion, but not of stillness ... Where is the life we have lost in living? Where is the wisdom we have lost in knowledge? Where is the knowledge we have lost in information?

These sterile state-funded rooms are probably just what the poet had in mind when he prophesised a moral and spiritual famine. Such an impasse is already here, played out daily in GP surgeries, NHS consultancy rooms and social services' meetings. We meet in these state-funded rooms as pawns in our respective hierarchies, not really knowing what's going on. At an earlier review a trainee mental health nurse volunteered to take notes. She is at one of the lower tiers of state psychiatric care, an initiate in one of the nation's protected hierarchies. Her life and how it pans out in the years and decades ahead depend on how she plays her cards in the coming hours and days. With enough long and emotionally draining shifts and enough jumps through the right hoops, she will move onto the next level. Remuneration will improve. There will be the material and professional comforts of a middle-class life to look forward to, a mortgage and an adequate car to drive, foreign getaways and nights out in town. In time she could even go on to become a senior community psychiatric nurse or a practice manager. She takes an interest in her notetaking, an eye on the longer game. Who'd blame her?

The psychiatrist is a prince of his hierarchy, invested with credentials from The Royal College of Psychiatry and with the right sequence of letters after his name. It's a struggle for him not to come across as smug. His diagnoses and prescriptions are authorized by law, approved by pharmaceutical and medical hierarchies, by the state and by subsidiaries of the state. Maybe we could even view him as a protégé of a number of vested interests in the state. Why wouldn't he come across as smug? The power dynamic is tilted in his favour. Yet we live in dangerous times so if the psychiatrist goes out on a limb and says or does anything rash there might well be consequences.

There are enough ambulance-chasing, no-win no-fee lawyers out there to cause even a prince of the psychiatric hierarchy to lose a little sleep at night, worrying if the right words were said at the right moments. So he asks a number of questions but answers none, inserting unhelpful silences into the half an hour allocated to the mental health outpatient in question. Language skills and interpersonal skills are as useful as drugs in most of the statutory powers of state psychiatry.

When our thoughts turn towards the psychiatrist aren't our thoughts turning towards a mere mortal who is as interested as we are in the improvement of mental disorder? Such idealism comes in second place to the important stuff. When piecing together the Western version of the universal shaman before us, we find lots of input from parents and extended family. Unfulfilled ambition of parents animates the man sitting before us. Investment from his family in his education and in his medical degree has brought him here, and he carries them with him in his every move and gesture. It is naïve to think that the psychiatrist is here as a representative of his own professional wisdom and acumen. There are others here with him. His family of origin are here in the room with us as much as the last communiqués he had from the Royal College of Psychiatrists. His wife or partner, financial advisor, and dependents are here too, symbolising earnings and out-goings for the coming years. Are we really waiting for such a crowded personage to say or to do anything outside the box?

Looked at holistically, or realistically if that word is more acceptable, there is as much chance of the psychiatrist saying something unexpected during our allocated half an hour as there is of the mental health patient abruptly standing up to say he has finally worked out what his problem is and then walking out the door. Much like the trainee mental health nurse who volunteered to take notes, the psychiatrist is playing the long game. They too must survive in an often ruthless world and be seen to thrive in the eyes of those around them. They have internalised the biological methodology that underlies present-day psychiatry as a means of personal survival as much as anything else.

Pharmacology is present in the room too, much like the taint of sulphur during a midnight medieval dalliance. It is impossible to avoid its aura anywhere near the annexes and walkways of modern-day psychiatric care. During any of these allocated half-hours there is never time to mention a growing anti-medication lobby within the community of mental health outpatients and legally informed advisors. Time is gutted skilfully and served up like a tasteless kipper. Faced with such formidable and multi-layered obstacles in the care and support of those suffering from chronic mental anguish, a more holistic approach that includes spiritual ideas can seem like a negotiation with the impossible, or near-impossible.

The mental health outpatient at the centre of this precious half hour is a gentle guy from a gentle family who had his life ruined by mental illness at a formative age when the more serious conditions often manifest. For the sake of the exercise let's call him Frank. After a series of dramas in late teenage years he spent all his twenties in mental hospitals, limped through his thirties in mental health residential projects of one grade or other, and now, having just turned forty, is settled into a routine in a residential care-home specialising in acute mental illness. What's referred to as the positive symptoms of Frank's schizophrenia are quite subdued by the profundity of the schism between his engagement with the world around him and his inner world. His voices too are muted, mostly existing as part of a secret world with Frank as the only initiate into its workings. He says little about his voices; says little about most things in fact.

Pythagoras was said by Diogenes Laertius to have lived five previous lives that he could remember in detail. From Heraclides Ponticus we learn that these past lives were lived as Aethalides the son of Hermes, Euphorbus, a hero mentioned in the *Iliad*, the philosopher Hermotimus, a fisherman by the name of Pyrrhus and a beautiful courtesan. Who would be brave or innocent enough to mention any credible link between Frank's voices and the hypothesis of previous lives, in a world of career-mindedness, business model conformity, and obeisance to the secular gods of pharmacology and cognitive science? There's holism and there's naïvety after all. And, among serious people, who wants to be viewed as naïve?

Frank is on a high daily dose of anti-psychotic medication and such meds are also classed as major tranquilisers. So, between the numbing effects of medication and the cognitive schism of his mental health condition, he can appear at quite a distance from what most of us look upon as normal social interaction. He takes his time to reply to questions—a minute or maybe two minutes. It takes a stretch of many hours over many days to enter his world of quietude and slow-release reactions to the world around him. After the extraordinary length of time Frank takes to answer the psychiatrist's opening question, the psychiatrist's body language speaks of an even lesser interest in the afternoon's review.

Modern, clinical responses to the dilemmas of ordinary people can come across as needlessly reductive, cautious, and non-committed. Actually throwing a value judgement on the table can be seen as a major failing. Dissipation in trust brought about by a compensation/liability culture has largely brought us here. Somewhere along the line this psychiatrist, struggling to stay fully awake in the afternoon, most likely said something during a review, ward-round or consultation that found its way back to him through an unofficial route. A colleague, maybe an NHS Trust Manager or a supervising psychiatrist, might have mentioned it in a friendly little aside. It would not have come across as a rebuke, just a friendly word or two thrown in among the usual banter of the day. But the psychiatrist took it in and, because he took it in, he is more careful about what he says.

The finer points of Frank's take on the world are passed over without mention. In the grammar of state psychiatry, the necessary boxes are ticked. The client presents as okay, is cared for, accommodated and supported by a specialist care-home. He is compliant with his medication and has no significant issues with physical health or medication side-effects. Next. Even if we had the time who would dare mention Frank's interest in UFOs? It's a sign of mental instability so must be ignored or passed over with the briefest smile of understanding. The fact that a recent survey showed that 36% of Britons believe in extra-terrestrials with 35% undecided must be ignored too. UFO sightings have also increased, from hundreds in 1990 to thousands in the 2020s.

Psychiatric medicine doesn't believe in such things even if millions of ordinary people do. Hence they are not mentioned. Psychiatry is a significant hierarchy, after all, and the first rule of hierarchies is to fortify their privileges. And taking UFOs seriously does not fortify the psychiatry hierarchy. There is a lot at stake, remember, and not just the improvement of Frank's diagnosis and quality of life. In fact, Frank's life and its ups and downs are incidental to what is at stake. There are a million Franks who come and go, but there are only a few noteworthy hierarchies in the mental health world, and their survival and advancement supersede any of the individual cases subject to the hierarchy's whims, rules, cultural nuances, moods, values, and dictates. This is a most obvious fact but is often brushed aside by public relations, the pace of events in fast-moving societies, and cultural norms set in place over many generations.

The case of Emil Schwyzer, also referred to as the "Solar-Phallus man", was an inspiration for Jung's formative thoughts on what he would go onto cultivate as his theory of the "collective unconscious". Jung came across Schwzyer, who'd been diagnosed with schizophrenia, staring, or we might say squinting, at the sun. When Jung asked Schwzyer what he was doing he replied that he was looking at the sun's penis which caused the winds to blow. Later Jung came across a Mithraic liturgy, part of the Greek Magical Papyri published in 1910, where a ministering wind was said to come from an adjunct jutting out from the sun.

As a clerk without the advantage of a third-level education, it was thought unlikely that Schwyzer would have known about the Mithraic liturgy, which in any case was published in 1910, which was after he was said to have made his remarks about the sun's penis. There's been revision regarding the reliability of events as remembered by Jung, and it seems that Schwyzer actually spoke to Jung's student Johann Honegger about what he'd seen. The dates and locations vary from account to account, as does Schwyzer's knowledge of mythology. But what can be said is that Schwyzer, suffering from schizophrenia and treated at a psychiatric hospital, reported what he saw, and Jung found it meaningful enough to use it as a foundation stone in one of his primary theories.

What can be said for sure about Frank's review is that there'll be no discussion of his interest in UFOs, no investigation into what such an interest might mean in relation to his diagnosis. Under the ethos imposed by pharmaceutical clout, all such speculation is delusional and cannot be encouraged. After all Frank is thought-disordered and probably prone to hallucinations. There is no time for such things anyway. Medicate. Comply. Move on. Those involved are caught up in economic servitude and the pressures such servitude brings, so we must keep up the masquerade too. If asked about Jung's wider enquiries into such things, a psychiatrist or psychiatric nurse connected with Frank's case would probably say something like:

> Jung must have had more time on his hands than we have.

Frank says he doesn't hear voices. But that doesn't mean the spiritual parasites that researchers like Jerry Marzinsky and Wilson Van Dusen claim infest the psyches of those who hear voices are not present.

They may have become so much a part of his thought processes that he's not aware that they are separate from his own thoughts. High daily doses of potent psychotropic medication sedate his consciousness so that it would be harder for him to differentiate the patterns of thinking within his mind. And not enough trust has been built up between him and anyone insightful enough to grasp what is going on. If Frank did trust someone enough to share what is going on in his mind, it may become known to the team that he does experience voices. One-to-one work could then begin to identify these voices, to isolate them and even over time expunge them from Frank's being. That might be the spirt work needed to reduce his medication, since the entities that intrude on his conscious mind can appear to be of a spiritual nature; entities actualised from deeper mind.

Another point we probably won't touch on in the meeting is Frank's interest in religious phenomena. Not only in the mental health sector but throughout much of society, there is no will, space or time to discuss religion. Often it's a dualistic weighing up of the two polarised extremes, with bitter, disappointing, or coercive childhood experiences of mainstream religious indoctrination thrown in as an ending to whatever exchange of ideas takes place. Yet there are many seekers, free-thinkers, mystics, scholars, seers, esoteric Christians, purveyors of the mushroom, and Taoists who don't confine themselves to narrow historically prejudicial, and literalist readings of accepted scripture. There are even those who ponder on the 2nd Century Gnostic Valentinius's concept of thirty-six archons, and the thirty-sixth as the only female archon Sophia, who gave birth, through a disastrous incestuous love, to Yahweh the ignorant creator of the Book of Genesis. Yahweh's ignorance is linked to the ignorance of so much in the human record but beyond this woeful demiurge is a scintilla—the light of a higher God within reach of humanity.

What forums are there for Frank or indeed for any of us to talk about certain ideas, to submerge our thoughts in mythology and teleology lost in the byways of ancient history, rather than in a literalist cast of polarised religious characters? We could open doors for a guy like Frank by linking his personal experiences with higher sacral notions. Psychiatry views religion with suspicion, as often little more than a control mechanism. Yet doesn't psychiatry operate as a control mechanism? There is a sense that the bored psychiatrist taking today's review would reply to speculations on Frank's religious yearnings in the spirit of counter-cultural guru Timothy Leary, although Leary was talking about a different kind of medication:

> When in doubt, double the dose.

The profundity of Frank's disordered mind is such that it's hard to work out if he is content or discontented at any given moment, or sad or not particularly sad. He is out of synch with the culture he is part of. There is a world of imagery, sensation and language of one kind or another that he's privy to and that he doesn't wish to share with others. Or maybe it's a question of trust.

Italian psychiatrist Silvano Arieti was one of the pioneers of psychoanalysis in psychiatry. His slimmest publication, *The Parnas: A Scene from the Holocaust* first published in 1979, takes us to the Jewish experience in Pisa during the Second World War. Arieti is leaving the horrors of Hitler's vision for Europe and is bidding farewell to the Parnas, the president of Pisa's only synagogue. The ageing Parnas's kindness, generosity, and humanity very much influenced the young Arieti, not least because of an enduring mental condition that mostly limited the Parnas to a life lived indoors. The Parnas had a chronic fear of animals, particularly dogs. When he occasionally went outside he swung a cane behind him as he walked to ward off imaginary dogs. This kind-hearted elder and guardian of the temple at Pisa touched the heart of Arieti, and knowing him was a motivation in Arieti's choice of psychiatry as his medical speciality. From the Parnas Arieti learned

> … to see the mentally ill patient not simply to cure or to pity—that is, as someone whose assertions are not to be taken quite seriously—but as a person who, in addition to his illness, or in spite of his illness, may have profound insight or wisdom to offer … I have been able to reflect on how much I have learnt from mental patients, not just about illness, but about life itself.

Arieti's humanism is elucidated in his book *Interpretations of Schizophrenia* which won the 1955 National Book Prize for science in America. His psychodynamic humanist approach lost out over time to brain-science experimentalists who see the problem first and foremost in terms of atoms, neutrons, and DNA codes. Arieti would hardly recognise today's psychiatrists who are seen from so many angles as generously remunerated representatives of the pharmaceutical conglomerates holding sway over not just psychiatry but almost all western medical practice. The thought association that comes to mind is "psychiatrist = control mechanism".

Arieti saw that a glut of medication renders patients impassive, numbed, and less open to insight-related work. Such valuable work has long been subsumed by closures of residential settings where dynamic interventions over a span of time were at least feasible, by the ascendency of pharmacology, and by reductive cognitive science which leaves inner worlds of creativity and imagination untouched. And we must also mention the deinstitutionalisation programmes which have removed so many of the basics needed for personal survival. Silvano Arieti would have much to say to a guy like Frank because he would be open to learning from whatever Frank had to say. He would not be satisfied with the higher doses of anti-psychotic medication, which we must remember are also major tranquilisers, and a treatment plan that's little more than a box-ticking exercise.

Frank comes across as wholly unmoved by his yearly review, with nothing to say about this annual half an hour under the eye of a state psychiatrist. He won't get into any kind of conversation about it, and has nothing whatsoever to say on the matter. There is a sense that even by the starkly reductive standards of state psychiatry he thinks this year's half an hour was even worse than last year's. There is not much humanity in such meetings, much less holistic opportunity for inner work leading to inner transformation. They are low-energy, often depressing, exercises and are probably intended to be so.

The Western shaman stands before their clients stripped of magic and with a juju bag bulging with spirit-killing pills that in the long term guide the soul towards darkness rather than light. A Trickster with a tarot deck and a crazy grin, and with a full half an hour devoted to the fortune of another, might at least draw a word or two out from a guy like Frank. Laying down major and minor arcana cards from a Tarot de Marseille deck, he might coax Frank from a hidden sanctum to the world of human interaction for even a short minute or two. Such an alternative half an hour might be therapeutic or could hardly be less therapeutic than the annual review. Josée Contreras, along with the ethnologist Jeanne Favret-Saada and an unnamed cartomancer, put forward the thesis that cartomancy, divining through cards, works much like therapy. For aren't the cards not so much about the future but more about the present and finding acceptance of the present?

In a reductive reading of Frank's life, and so many others like him, it's a case of bad luck viewed through a series of random causal factors. He went into the transformations of adolescence and early adulthood, but did not come out the other side in a fit psychic state to take on the challenges of a highly competitive and aggressive age. There was no sacrifice of time and brainpower leading to exceptional exam results and a call to the citadels of higher education. No science prize either for a final year project on protein analysis or gene sequencing, no molecular biology degree as a route into the chimpanzee genome project. There was no invitation to join the Human Genome Project either, nor was there a high-status job offer in the biotech industry or in some such industry feted by the movers and shakers of a culture under the spell of innovators in materialist science.

Instead, there were glum medical appointments, cognitive deterioration, social withdrawal, self-neglect, a falling behind in competitive areas, a paucity of ideas, and a mother's private tears. As others went on to accomplish things in the world as it stands, Frank and a legion of fellow-travellers only found satisfaction in hidden sanctums of mind. After more medical observation, followed by psychiatric reviews, Frank and so many others passed into a categorisation under the general banner of "schizophrenia".

In R.D Laing's *The Undivided Self* we find a dismal analysis by the brilliant but flawed psychiatrist:

> The schizophrenic is desperate, is simply without hope. I've never known a schizophrenic who could say he was loved, as a man, by God the Father or by the Mother of God, or the Devil, or in Hell, estranged from God. When someone says he is an unreal man or that he is dead, in all seriousness, he is expressing in radical terms the stark truth of his existence as he experiences it, that is—insanity.

For Laing, schizophrenia is synonymous with a wider existential darkness, and his remedies are based on reinterpretations of standard models such as "insane" and "sane" and a sharper awareness of loneliness and difference. But the schism in Frank's cognitive functionality is such that we don't know if he thinks he is God or the Devil or if he is in hell.

With Frank, communication is always the first casualty of his condition. As one of the care workers observed in passing:

> Frank doesn't say much. He's like a shell really.

This is the reality of the condition known as schizophrenia with its injurious costs in the lives of those it afflicts. Frank shares with millions alive today and with those who lived in earlier times a fragmentation of personality that situates him down on the lower rungs of achievement, engagement, and actualisation in the world.

The trainee mental health nurse taking notes is struggling to hide her yawns behind a series of hand gestures. She looks exhausted, rings of fatigue already showing under her young eyes. The spiritual parasites found in schizophrenia that mainstream psychiatry describes as hallucinations consume the energy of the unfortunate person whom they are living off and also those they come into contact with. They exhaust their host with tirades and then consume the negative energy created by their presence. The energy of mental health workers is also consumed by these parasites, leaving workers feeling utterly fatigued at shift's end. In keeping with a present-day psychological paradigm, these parasites could originate from the Jungian unconscious.

> The unconscious is an autonomous psychic entity; any efforts to drill it are only apparently successful, and moreover are harmful to consciousness. It is and remains beyond the reach of subjective, arbitrary control, in a realm where nature and her secrets can never be improved upon nor perverted, where we can listen but may not meddle.
>
> (C.G Jung. *Psychology and Alchemy*)

There is something about mental illness that's so familiar or personal that almost everyone claims to have ideas worth listening to about the subject. Maybe the line between functional mental health and dysfunctional mental health is so fluid and so brittle that this should be expected. The redefining of so many categories of psychological disorder leads to novel conceptualisations of what mental illness or mental disorder actually is. What were for millennia marked off as the unavoidable sufferings of human existence are reclassified as psychological or psychiatric conditions. In the times where we find ourselves, we are unsure if we are suffering because of our humanity or if we are dogged by a psychological or psychiatric condition with a curative pathway that most likely involves prescribed synthetic medication tagged onto it.

If what those who went before us understood as the to-be-expected suffering of life, is now reinterpreted as psychological or psychiatric disorder, then what other questions beg to be asked? Is the line between acute mental dysfunction and manageable mental dysfunction a matter of what people can take and deal with on a daily basis? Running such a line of inquiry to a conclusion, might there be an argument for accepting that those who can handle suffering can avoid psychological diagnoses? To begin from the baseline of holism and spirit work is to ask every reasonable question there is to ask.

In conversations through the years with a number of people with neurotic tendencies, it came across that they often found it easier to come to terms with their difficulties in life when they were diagnosed with a psychological condition. They struggled to dissect their own suffering from the suffering of others. Empathy with others was limited. They would not wish to spend more than a few seconds thinking about those with enduring psychiatric illnesses. Not that wishing to avoid thinking about the suffering of others is rare, but these individuals with neurotic characteristics had quite an aversion to it. They also often believed they suffered just as much if not more so than psychiatric patients in acute wards but that such patients had certain symptoms such as hallucinations which brought them more attention. Grudgingly they'd concede that the chronic hospital cases needed care before quickly refocusing attention back to their own issues and suffering. Empathy fatigue had set in before there were any first signs of empathy.

Care for the mentally disordered is tempered by our own suffering and by our own estimation of who qualifies for sympathetic care and who doesn't. These considerations, among others, are but the beginning of the journey into the lives of others. Like most things that appear straightforward, caring for the mentally disordered, in care homes or in what is referred to without irony as the community, is not straightforward at all. On paper at least we have a system of care which is adequately administered, legally framed, and monitored. But politics, funding defaults, human complexity, and limitations on emotional resources often lead to far different outcomes than were hoped for.

Standards of care and support in modern advanced societies are inspired by intimate family relationships. Those employed to care are asked to offer the highest standards, as if they are caring for someone who is part of their own family or intimate circle. To offer such a consistent level of care, while at the same time keeping the boundaries so often spoken about by social workers and social care regulators, is just one tension in the administration of care for the mentally disordered. If we can begin by factoring in all these points and condensing them into a here-and-now emphasis, then we are living in the moment. Now we have a reasonable hope of helping others to overcome phobias and morbidities that are so often centred in abstractions stuck in the past, but are projected into the future or into a parallel or private world unknown to the outsider. And to the person caught up in a crisis of mental aberration, we are all outsiders.

Another tension is equality, since even the briefest survey of recently published Employment Tribunal findings based on discrimination of one kind or another confirms that such outcomes are not in a hurry to go away. As far as we can see, what is known as the Voluntary Sector—which takes a leading role in the care and support of the mentally disordered as well as the NHS and its co-working agencies—has a permenant presence at Employment Tribunal hearings. Notwithstanding assurances from overly remunerated senior managers and politicians, we find it hard to get even the basics right.

In beginning a journey into the National Health Service and its co-working partners' engagements with the mentally disordered, it is a mistake to believe it will be any less tense or fraught with underlying themes of harassment, prejudice, incompetence, corruption and cruelty than any other sector. When taking a closer look at Frank's condition and the importance of medication in all statutory work with him, a number of points must be re-stated. Firstly, there will never be a drug to cure depression or anxiety disorders just as there will never be a drug to cure discrimination against minorities, hatred of others based on their characteristics, or bigotry towards the disabled. The problem is generally not centred on genetics but rather on modelling, as parents, families, communities, and state regulators cannot pass on what they themselves are lacking. Secondly, the focus needs to be less on the unchangeable past and more on the present and immediate future. Thirdly, no amount of medication can bring into being successful stress-management techniques, plausible self-explanatory narratives, skills to build and maintain positive relationships, and flexible, discriminating cognitive skills. Medication cannot do any of these things just as it cannot teach people useful problem-solving skills and decision-making strategies, or how to transcend an adverse personal history and build and maintain a constructive support network, which in doing will open up roads to a realistic and motivating future. Moving on from Frank and his annual review, a number of questions are tagged onto so many unanswered questions. None of this is for the faint-hearted or those with poor health. The challenges are substantial. Not all are drawn to the world of mental health work and holism. These pages are dedicated to those who are.

Tina

It's one of those grey mornings in London when it ought to be cold but isn't. Inuit elders have reportedly been in touch with NASA as they have noticed that the earth has wobbled off its axis. The sun doesn't rise where the sun used to rise before. Is this it? Is this misalignment messing up the world's weather? In this present stage of evolution are we yet capable of tuning into wisdom from outside technological innovation and hyper-consumerism, from somewhere that doesn't orbit around the loneliness and vulnerability of the solitary consuming unit? Whatever it is, it's warm in late November when it should be cold.

I am on my way to see a forty-one-year-old woman who is drinking herself to death. The statutory health authorities and the local mental health trust have seemingly given up on her. As a social worker spelt out to me on the phone, the patient in question, let's call her Tina, already had two alcohol detox admissions over a ten-month period. At four and a half thousand pounds per detox it's about her mark for the year. Anyhow, the social worker added, it clearly doesn't work. Tina is off to the off-licence as fast as her weakened legs can take her, as soon as she gets out through the doors of the detox ward.

As someone employed by a mental health charity, part of the voluntary sector component of deinstitutionalisation, I have somehow got to come up with a remedy or two for Tina. I would like to suggest that all of us, charity workers, mental health outpatients, alcoholics, psychiatrists, and psychiatric nurses get together one evening and take a microdose of something suitably hallucinogenic on an empty stomach and then talk about where the trip took us and what solutions are then possible. Of course, if I did mention such a thing at the team meeting or in an email, they would take it as a joke. What else could they do but think I'm joking?

There's an unspeakable smell in the downstairs hallway of the house where Tina lives. An image of a thousand dead mice rotting under greasy carpets creeps to mind. Before I hurried from the office I rang Tina's GP. She said bluntly that it is pointless bringing her to see them. The GP was even blunter when she said that there is nothing they can do for her. If there are any miracles or cures today they will have to come from either me or Tina, or from somewhere unconnected to the pragmatism of the National Health Service. "Good luck", the doctor added without any apparent sarcasm in her voice.

I didn't say anything but I wanted to mention the sisterhood we hear so much about, the solidarity of female with female. Surely identity politics have meaning around here. Surely the female doctor could have made just a bit more effort. Tina is a female too after all. Maybe she is the wrong kind of female, or a female with all the wrong causal factors attached to her presenting predicament. Or maybe she is just too poor and sick and unimportant and has no social media followers and absolutely no hope of ever making it to a protest to hold up a confrontational placard, or tweet a striking signature of virtue to the right set of followers. Or maybe the kind of feminism they encourage in a number of universities and in the strands of media fired up by the revolution yet to come is not what we are led to believe it is. Maybe it's just another theory dreamed up among self-congratulating intellectuals with not much going on in their lives that hardly even touches on the reality of the human condition as we find it. Whatever it is it's not helping Tina.

There is a real sense of an absence of goodness here. If we had a Kirlian camera and used it to photograph Tina what would her aura look like? In these squalid rooms so many hours of neglect and poor health are hard to pin down in real terms, hard to see objectively. The underlying meaning of it all is not obvious. Devoid of light from a conscious sun it can read as evil, a sense of stepping into a place of evil.

In popular evolutionary theory the human brain and its attributes are said to have evolved as a consequence of biological survival rather than as an urge to understand the nature of reality. We are survivors and competitors, say the post-Darwinist theorists, not philosophers. How do we escape the conclusion that we cannot fathom our own reality by using rationality alone? The human mind just isn't configured to work out the totality of primary facts and the origins of the human condition. At best the rational mind can grasp what it is to be part of a given society or culture, or to reconcile, to a certain extent, literalist creeds spun by a cult or sect or creed or great religion with a given way of living in a certain time. I am halfway up the stairs to Tina's room when the biological limitation of our minds becomes more immediate. Who can claim to comprehend the misery of this house and the struggles of those living here?

We are no different from any other civilisation or culture in our need to make sense of the universe and our place in it. The detachment of nature from the cosmos and what the cosmos might mean does not help us: that old spiel lifted from now less confident readings of literalist monotheistic scripture that hoists us up to where we are lords over the natural world rather than a part of it. How much lonelier can it get? In a cosmos stripped of mythology and magic the modernist who is not religious or God-conscious in a personal way is as irrelevant as eddies of dust on a faraway planet. How empty the materialist view is when stripped of mythos and mystery, reduced to hollow soundings from a radio telescope aimed perpetually at a mute sky. Cosmically our lives are blinkered by so many new variations of an old, dogged scientism and by a poignant helplessness that doesn't seem in any hurry to lessen its hold on the imagination.

The assertions of practically all the secular western institutions that the cosmos is mechanical, that everything is inside our heads, that immutable laws of nature magically came into existence because of a theory known as the Big Bang, are counterintuitive to most people in tune with their senses. It is not the common experience to conceptualise the night sky as mechanistic and devoid of meaning. Yet this is what we are told to believe by a scientific hegemony bloated by public money. The materialist philosophy squatting so stubbornly on the Western soul props up so many of these dystopian walkways, these godless and pharmaceutically oppressed avenues of protracted misery.

Transcendence couldn't live here in this house of multiple occupation. It is an interior wedded to nihilistic views of humankind as blindly determinist, essentially hopeless and ugly. It is a mirroring of the German realist philosopher Schopenhauer's will to live, the indifference of a force driving on a multitude of species to survive even when there's little sense or comfort in surviving. For Schopenhauer

> ... all the cruelty and torment of which the world is full is in fact merely the necessary result of the totality of the forms under which the will to live is objectified, and thus merely a commentary on the affirmation of the will to live.

At certain moments, like setting foot in the house of rented rooms where Tina lives, it would be nice to have a little cosmological or universal truth to pass on. Can the theory of a Big Bang from prehistory bring a little comfort to these doorsteps of misery? Secular prejudice makes it harder to look hopefully to religion or mysticism, if they have any bearing at all in our lives. All the clever people forsake such things and the educated, we are told, completely believe in materialist science. It is easier to talk about the weather or the football or what was on television last night.

If we have any status in the hierarchies that make up human societies then we can embrace it, use it to keep the more gruesome torments of life at arm's length. Or there might be a social or political cause or meaning pure enough for us to run with for years or even decades. Usually on the doorsteps of the consistently poor and troubled, any sense of meaningfulness is spread thin, or isn't there at all. For the mental health worker at the crossroads of good and evil it is easy to say the wrong thing or to use an optimistic inflection of voice at the wrong time.

Tina is waiting at the top of the stairs as it's usually as far as she is fit to go. On good days she gingerly limps on swollen feet to the high street to buy cigarettes and alcohol. Mostly she is dependent on her partner as he brings the alcohol and collects her vitamin prescriptions. She's forty-one but looks twenty years older. Her eyes are shadowed by dark lines as if a malignant hand has daubed her with a bluish black paste.

Is it plausible to believe that the human organism can adapt to evolutionary requirements for survival in a changing environment? If we are born with an *a priori* mechanism for adapting to our conditions in this world, would it really inflict on itself the suffering of this world? Isn't it more believable that a force or intelligence outside the human organism is compelling us to adapt in order to survive? If the evolutionary engine for constant adaptation is propelled solely from the human organism, would that organism be so willing to surrender to conditions it finds baffling and so often discomforting? Surely the popularised concept of evolution must be fixed by an external force, because a self-regulating organism by its very orientation must spring back in horror from an evolutionary ordeal of prolonged and at times barely tolerable levels of boredom and suffering.

When we look at humanity in its totality, can we see it as in any way improved from earlier peaks of civilisation? Have we really evolved? There are societal and technological improvements and signs of biological evolution in the fossil record, but we've lived under the threat of nuclear annihilation since 1945 with nuclear warheads primed and pointed in a thousand apocalyptic directions. Is this the sign of an evolved species? Is the squalor of Tina's home any indication of progressive evolution? If we rethink for a moment the accepted theories of how and why the pyramids at Giza were constructed, the rational mind can only marvel at the civilisations of the ancients.

Linked to a global pattern of pyramids, the pyramids at Giza in their innovative splendour were configured by minds demonstrably more agile in comparison to so many who came after them. Accepting all the gaps in our historical knowledge of those who built the pyramids, it is harder now to believe that we have any real connection with such civilisations. The birth and death of civilisations in a cyclical manner leaves us clinging to half-truths and wearier conclusions. Influential voices in the pseudo-religion of materialist science and its secular offshoots proclaim a biological primacy in evolution, when in reality there are yet more question marks added to those that are already there.

Humankind's record in mass killing and in mutating the natural world in attempts to control it rules out a hypothesis of progressive evolution. Such thoughts are sharper here in this house of squalor and pain. Lofty, often arrogant pronouncements of progress carry no weight here or in so many other similar places. Here, the idea of human progress is at best academic, at worse a joke at someone else's expense.

On the short walk up the stairs and through a dark and bad smelling corridor to the room Tina shares with her partner, someone is playing music in one of the rooms or flats at the back of the house. It's an old song from a sentimental radio station: *Love Letters Straight from the Heart*.

There is an innocence in how the singer emotes the lyrics, changing the vulgar interior to one where the only meaningful use of time is remembering our first love or first erotic kiss. If music conjoined with words has the power to change the mood of a place like this, then its power is awesome and unknowable.

Whatever we might think about ideas of evolutionary progress Tina seems pleased to have a visitor. She reaches out in friendliness and solidarity. In the bonds of simple conversation we create a connection, superseding this impasse in her life which confronts us both in different ways. We might be anywhere at any time, friends meeting or acquaintances passing each other on just another mundane rat-run and pausing to talk. Nothing in Tina's friendliness and unaffected sensitivity belongs here. What is the nature of the external energy driving her on? The presence of a sympathetic person in the slum of her home locates her in the here-and-now. Phantoms of the past or terrors from the future are strangers to the passing moments.

Stalin's Soviet dystopia insisted on an official version of reality that had to be mimicked by the people. Everyone knew it was all phony but for personal survival those living under Stalin's rule parroted the mistruths, distortions of truth, and outright lies. Historians looking back at those decades offer the explanation that the exceptional efforts by Stalin's regime to force entire populations to swallow and then express a version of reality they knew to be false were intended to demoralise the people. A demoralised people would be more controllable and less likely to resist. There is a parallel in these present times where a materialist philosophy permeates the culture and coerces populations to believe in a reductive world view that is alarming in its intellectual paucity and nihilistic in its implications.

Maybe it is little more than a useful creed for the consumerist mania that we now see everywhere, a despairing dirge to urge populations to consume even more and to find a meaning in life in the act of consumption itself. If there is no God, if the cosmos is not vital, if we are little more than automatons without volition, if our reality can be reduced to a dissected brain on a mortuary slab, then why not consume until the very end of what there is to consume? Any culture that encourages its citizens to trade their own subjective experiences of the world for a materialist philosophy that is promoted as an alternative to faith and culture aligns itself with dystopias answerable for the physical deaths of millions and the spiritual deaths of hundreds of millions.

The Journal of Humanistic Psychology edited by Abraham Maslow set out approaches to the human dilemma in the hope of prioritising human dignity. Maslow's emphasis was on a sequence of rights: the right to satisfy needs, express emotions, vindicate feelings; the right to be different, unique, and specific; the right to be fulfilled and to conform to individual, social, and spiritual values but not be limited by the will of others. Looking around the living spaces of people like Tina who are signed up to our mental health charity, it is hard to miss the disconnect between the praiseworthy work of so many humanists and the reality of the mental health sufferer in crisis or the alcoholic in the advanced stages of E Morton Jellinek's alcoholism. How many pieces of the jigsaw are actually missing?

The human is a child of the spiritual part of one or other of the glorious suns scattered through frontierless space. So wrote the Theosophist Dr. Gottfried de Purucker. "Ye are gods in your inmost parts—atoms of some spiritual sun." An unstated directive in Tina's medical prognosis hints that the gods within or the atoms she shares with de Purucker's spiritual sun are her only real hope. It could be heard in the doctor's voice during our phone conversation, her helplessness in the face of acute alcoholism. If the GP and her colleagues sectioned the severe alcohol cases and treated them voluntarily and involuntarily they would burn out their yearly budget inside a bank holiday weekend. The sharpest minds in medicine and psychology are stumped by alcoholism in its most merciless manifestations. If there is an answer it must be buried somewhere inside Tina's own neurological programming or pathology, or in some other direction not ordinarily spoken of. What spirit work is possible must be preceded by a world of practicality.

We begin to unravel our way through the complexities of Tina's practical problems as she herself sees them. She talks about her partner and about his casual labouring and handyman work. She talks about his friends and contacts from the local pubs and how much they love him in one particular pub. She laughs when she mentions how after eight or nine drinks he breaks into a Gary Barlow number that's almost as good as the maestro himself. He means the world to her and, when she mentions his name, the love in her eyes shines through.

There is enough banal work to get on with, government tick-boxes to be ticked and questionnaires to be filled in. We must find time for debt management and the many other petty humiliations in the lives of the poor. And then there's housing. The walls and ceiling of the dark room

Tina shares with her partner are heavily dappled in greenish, blackish damp. From halfway up the stairs the stench of rotting plaster makes breathing difficult. A strange, mushroom-like fungus is sprouting from the darkest corner of the ceiling. I have already taken Tina to the local council housing office to beg for rehousing but they couldn't have been more unmoved if they were made of stone.

London's councils, or administrative governments, are in gatekeeping mode. Gatekeeping, for the councils, simply translates as doing all they can to prevent people from making homeless applications for emergency housing, or applying for social housing. By law they are obliged to offer housing and support for citizens in need, but in reality they meet only a puny percentage of the overall need. I don't have it in my heart to put Tina through another miserable and humiliating visit to the homeless persons unit. We will have to find another way forward.

The private landlord resents spending money to treat the damp in the house. Other tenants in the building complained about the lack of repairs and maintenance to the local council's environmental health officer. The landlord hit back by evicting the tenants. They refer to it as revenge eviction in the newspapers and it is pretty vindictive. Take away the roof from above a person's head and it is hard not to take it personally.

A colleague's number shows on my phone. It's a brief call and it means I'll have to cut this visit to Tina short. Another vulnerable adult needs a visit. I know the guy in question and spent many a long hour listening to his disconnected, paranoid thoughts. His mental illnesses span several acute ward admissions, suicide attempts, and years of engagement with mental health services. With all respect to the experimental work of Dr. R.D. Laing, if there are hidden values in the illness we know as schizophrenia they can be very hidden indeed.

The universe is expanding. Cosmologists explain this as proof of what they call the Big Bang existing as an actual event in time. Other cosmologists argue that light could not have travelled to all corners of the universe in the time that the universe is thought to have existed. Dark spots untouched by light are at odds with the premise of all conditions sharing the same principle of uniformity of light. Hannes Alfven's plasma theory is an article of faith for others. Even if we accept the idea of a cosmological pendulum, and that cosmology swings between mythical and scientific interpretations, what reassurance can we find there? If we take a step back from these arguments, our accepted cosmology creeps into view as yet more detached and theoretical, our cosmologists forever caught up in long-winded guessing games. Who exactly are they helping? What human value is there to be had in cobbling together scientific projections such as multiverses?

In a cultural and anthropological sense, have the conclusions of our most honoured cosmologists lessened any of the angst in the modern mind? On the clearest night of the year, as we marvel at the stars, are we comforted in any way by the horizon problem or by the latest revelation to do with the speed of light? Space agency information is disconnected from our cultural and daily experiences. It adds to the data at our disposal but, separated from a socio-cultural or metaphysical narrative, it can only intensify our loneliness and our alienation. It can only add yet more mind-crucifying questions as to why we are here and what are the best ways for us to live.

Cosmologists and astrophysicists help us to marvel at the design of the cosmos of which we are a minute part, but most critically leave out moral significance and philosophical conclusions. We stare at the stars and see a meditation on our own loneliness, while at the same time a tribal eye from lands far from here sees the stars as the campfires of ancestors. What do space probes, satellites, and telescopes really add to our dilemma as a life-form, their data detached from knowledge of our purpose on this planet Earth? We share carbon iron with the birth of stars but news of our origins in the stars has not yet filtered through to the public.

Humanist psychology separates its methodologies into pathological and normal templates, interpreting the human being as an open classification part of universal systems and organisms. But Tina's alcoholism is too grotesque to mention in the same breath as humanism, existentialism, phenomenology, or any other word separated from the squalor of her life. Her tee-shirt rides up a little when she moves an arm to show the discolouration of the skin stretched by her swollen liver.

Tina is sitting on the edge of her bed stroking her liver through her dirty t-shirt. Can anything in our culture help her to understand or accept her suffering? The old religion and its variant sects can still bring age-old comforts to believers but the news from the pulpit is not encouraging. Multi-millionaire televangelists in $65 million private jets, and slicker versions of snake-oil salesmen, have dragged popularised Western Christianity down into bestial depths. They dupe the gullible and the broken-hearted into a shallow dream of greed and one-upmanship supposedly validated by one of the world's great religions. Tina couldn't afford one of their dvd and book introductory packages anyhow. I ask myself what spirit work can be done here.

Tina and her partner and their circle of friends live without religion and its secular offshoots, as a sacrifice to the age of science. Going back in time, we the ordinary people didn't separate magic from science and mythology from culture. It was done for us you could say, or done to us if you prefer. If we view religion as another creative force on a par with the creativity of the plastic arts, the history of film, or the heights of musical composition, it then becomes another existential comfort. And since when did humanity need less existential comfort?

A subculture of hyper-consumerism has already condemned Tina, as in its stark reasoning wealth is Nirvana and poverty is hell. The NHS has already marked her margins in terms of intervention. The feminist narrative is as abstract for Tina as the plasma theory is for lovers marvelling at the stars on a clear night. There are no sisters willing to walk with her on this avenue of anguish, just as there is no applause to be had here, no attention or social media followers, or tenure or step up in status, nothing in the unremitting reality of just illness and poverty. Hardly anyone knows Tina exists, and her suffering is compartmentalised in line with the age of the isolated individual.

As the system grinds onwards, she will sooner or later find herself on another waiting list for a hospital detox bed. Apart from her partner and a few friends who remember the good times, there aren't many standing on the sidelines waving her on. She will at least have some help from mental health charities. Confused by so many conflicting truths, idealists still probe in the darkness for miracles, in a time when people are lectured and reminded over again that miracles are just a childish fantasy.

I would like to stay longer with Tina, maybe take her out to the high street just to give her a break from the misery and dampness of her room. But there are more visits to crack on with, more practical mental health support work waiting behind the squalid thresholds of the consistently poor. A few minutes' walk from Tina's front door, the weather changes in the span of a short wait for the next bus. Rain falls on citizens now even more detached from the agrarian need for rain. What keeps us going, like Tina in her squalid room waiting in hope for another detox bed to save her life? Others standing at bus stops in the rain in slate-grey cities? In his book *The Tree of Life: A Study in Magic*, Israel Regardie defines an astral body as:

> … the subtle duplicate to which the physical body owes its continued existence and persistence.

Is this why we keep going, because our bodies have a spiritual double existing in an invisible realm empowering us with the will to push through the days of rain and sadness? Surely it can't be any of the more popularised readings of evolutionary theory driving us on. There is nothing there to explain why the human organism strives for survival in hellish or just about sufferable conditions. It must be something else. A blind, indifferent first cause redirects the mind from idealism towards a more reductive worldview and towards the sobering words of Schopenhauer and the author of *Ecclesiastes*. Is that it? How else can scientists and psychologists explain human motivation in ways acceptable to the rational mind?

In a hyper-consumerist age only hyper-consumerist versions of cures and simples are accepted by the sick and dying. If we tried hard enough, we might persuade an herbalist or shaman with first-hand experience of psilocybin, or an esoteric Christian healer or practised holistic therapist to come with us on our visits, to offer the patients of our mental health charity other ways of looking at and coping with their maladies. But the outpatients hate such an idea. All their lives they have only ever known the GP as shaman and the chemical offerings of the pharmaceutical hegemony as medicinal succour. They would feel cheated if offered anything less than another GP appointment and the prescription that goes with it, yet another blood-test or scan, or a visit to a senior shaman in the guise of a hospital consultant. Isn't it now noticeable that the health of entire populations is monopolised by a profit-fixated pharmaceutical cabal, administered by an army of GPs? Sickness of all types almost always go together with the automatic word association of a GPs waiting room or a casualty department. To speak of alternatives is to take on the role of social revolutionary or crank, to masquerade as something we are not, in the hope of isolating a moment where we can pass on truth that's seen as heresy.

On the bus to the next appointment, I make a call on Tina's behalf to the borough's statutory alcohol and drug team. It's not a straightforward business. NHS managers in the former hospital where the alcohol team is now based have designed a mostly automatic switchboard system, so anyone calling in can't ever get through to an actual person. The best hope is for whoever you are trying to connect finding your voicemail message and getting back to you at a later point. The last time there was a wait of three weeks to hear from the alcohol worker I had left a message for. But it felt like a victory when she returned the call.

Before I jump off at the stop closest to where I am going there's a little time for me to think about how we are cast into life without any conscious say in the circumstances of our births, and no knowledge of why we are here or where we are going. Our life on earth is sustained by a star we call the sun with a diameter of a million kilometres and at a distance of ninety-three million miles from us. Beyond the sun are stars several times larger, galaxies of mystery and anomalies of astrophysics, imponderable to the human mind. If there is any hope of clarity or solace surely it must lie in new interpretations of our cosmos and our place in its immensity. If we cannot uncover new interpretations, or older interpretations from the arcane, then what remains for us to do but to gaze at each other incomprehensibly, no closer to understanding our fundamental condition than at any other time since the ascendency of rational thought.

The macrocosm is so bewildering, it is understandable when people ignore it and live existentially. Thus heaven and hell are created anew every day in the stock markets of major cities, because heaven is wealth and hell is poverty. In the working boroughs of a more stressed age the illusion of equality of opportunity, social mobility, and the hope for wealth and success dims by the day. After years of what governance refers to as "austerity programmes" the very streets and buildings proclaim a lack of faith in the hyper-consumerist ethos and in its jaded promise that all can share in the materialist dream of ever-growing abundance. Suicides, homelessness, disability, and death by addiction leave deeper stains on the working boroughs. Racism, institutional greed, corruption, and violence remain as grave social evils. Psychiatric, psychological, and physical aberrations can in many cases be traced back to an uncompromising socio-economic environment, as much as to Freud's natural injustices that the esteemed doctor told us cannot be remedied.

Hierarchies have been around for a very long time, but this in itself does not limit the problems such hierarchies present. The will to exploit others for economic benefit, linked as it may be to biological determinants, has not by the looks of it weakened through the ages. The propagandist might even sometimes wake from a self-imposed nightmare, choking on their own words of endless optimism. Implications of a debt-laden age can send shivers to the soul of the modernist with one eye on tomorrow. We stand more alone and vulnerable than perhaps at any time since the Dark Ages. Rituals of birth and death are perfunctory, and in the urban fields of squalor nothing at times is recorded other than by the impassive hand of someone or other contracted by a local social services' department. The density of rules and bureaucratic idiocy repress the residue of the spontaneous human heart. Gaps in trust and common understanding between citizens and cadres of elected representatives are unacceptably wide. Is this freedom? And if it is freedom, what do the other options look like?

I run it through my mind as I catch bus after bus, train after train, traversing the working boroughs to connect with post-psychotic outpatients and the addicted. The concentrated misery of people caught up in this miasma is a world away from the standards of dignity and logic so many rationalists aspire to, or idealists who speak of progress campaign for. Endless interference from state agencies subverts the expectation of self-autonomy and personal growth set in motion by the success of liberal societies and the Western cultural revolution of the nineteen-sixties. Casualties of an overly optimistic and progressive age sleepwalk into dependency on the next prescription, the next social security payment, the next diagnosis or hospital appointment, and the next visit to the GP. Their power as sentient, functioning human beings is undermined by a corrosion of self-belief and a loss through the generations of personal skills and folk wisdom. Endless, often petty squabbles with the state's regulating tentacles aggravate such helplessness to the point where everything that can be questioned is questioned.

There is a lack of self-power at the root of all this state medicine and intervention. Somewhere down the line something happened to demoralise people and to leave them more open to the illusions of the times. Something always happens. Governmental and trans-governmental economic tinkering alienates the individual even further from existential truths fixing the boundaries of our human lives, from the assurances of childhood and the resilience of those who went before us. A lack of enlightenment, self-power, and a surfeit of knowledge are compounded by a dissipation in health brought on by overwork and stress.

The high toll on people's health in eternal efforts to keep pace in a starker age of loneliness, technological alienation, fear, and job insecurity is now more fully documented. Or citizens fall into a mental health dysfunction brought on by a rat race they don't understand or really believe in. Or they fall into the boon companion of the post-industrial states, addiction.

If somehow the actual truths of existence are mirrored back to the human soul again and again, they surely must penetrate the tormented conscience struggling with even the most stubborn of illusions. They must get past the delusion of mental disorder and past the spiritual malaise born from dependency on state agencies. Such truths can even slip through the wrong thinking of decades and precipitate a eureka moment.

A manager rings me before I make it to the next doorstep of despair. He wants several risk assessments all done by the end of the week, with each assessment involving two to three hours of monotonous work in front of a computer. I tell him I have quite a few visits to make and a number of appointments and meetings with co-working agencies. It is unlikely I'm going to have the time to complete the assessments by the end of the week. It's not optional, he says. The paper-trail must be expanded by the week's close. There are no ifs or buts about it.

The manager is a nice guy. None of this is his doing. He was happily working as a club DJ in his mid-forties when he met a younger woman who quickly got pregnant. Now past fifty he has a wife and young child at home, and his wife doesn't work because of exorbitant childcare costs. Whatever the mental health charity asks him to do he does without question. It's just the system, the way things are. People get caught up in economics and sacrifice so often on the altar of employment. It's nothing personal, just how it goes.

Something one of the founders of Gestalt Therapy said about the ego comes across as even more truthful in these present days. It was Fritz Perls and he was talking about egoism:

> In egoism, the neurotic is aware and has something to say about everything, but the concentrating self feels empty, without need or interest.

It happens. Mental health charity workers cast onto the streets of need without the resources necessary to tackle the work in hand become detached from their own psychological needs, functioning as emotional automata. And I am wondering if it's happening to me. I try to work out if I am overly focused on the needs of others while there is a gaping need the size of an average planet at the very core of my own existence.

The lassitude of the social care worker caught up in too many impossible tasks is to be expected. It is always there in the back of the mind—the dread of one morning waking up to burnout. On another bus-ride and another trek by foot from flat to flat to visit post-psychotic outpatients signed up to our mental health charity, the only hope is to follow a holistic codex freed from dogma, paperwork deadlines, and the wrong thinking of so many agencies of the state. An entire hierarchy may insist on reducing wellness and health to a psychological and psychiatric substratum of the fad of materialist scientism, but an entire hierarchy may be wrong.

Looking with a harder eye at both religious and humanist narratives, and listening to the atheist and the secular humanitarian, only one route forward makes any real sense. To live in a time stripped of ritual and the potentiality of transcendence seems inhuman and a kind of self-flagellation, a denial of the instinct to think outside the now very jaded illusions we are shepherded into and which mutate easily to nihilism, addiction, or depression. The new evolutionists are at their worse an inversion of the most intolerant proponents of literal monotheism in the darker days of witch-prickings and sectarian prejudice. There may be a place for such reductionism in a university debate or in some other odd corner removed from the tribulations of life, but it's wilfully cruel to bring such reductive thinking into the fields of suffering we enter every day as mental health workers.

Influential people in thrall to hyper-consumerism and its fellow-traveller of scientism see a problem with looking for answers outside the radical creeds of materialism, be it in Jungian analysis, eastern beliefs, the arcane, conversations with the mushroom, or through the monotheistic religions. The atheistic design and outlook of the hard sciences make it easier to downgrade all humanity into categories and then miss the value of the individual as a complex and changing entity working through intergenerational karma or faced with very real spiritual crises. Regardless of what others are doing or saying, it is yet possible to live an ethical life and to at least look towards the transcendent without cynicism. So many scientific-related and existentialist ideas gleaned from the business model of today are quite useless, as people need workable truths and practical wisdom that can be applied to the whole human dilemma, rather than be asked to fit in with the ambitions of persons unknown to us.

For the mental health worker on the doorsteps of despair, what comfort is there in the public voices of cosmologists, philosophers, commentators, and popular scientists? Suffering has a language of its own and interprets cruelty and indifference in the knowing nod of the cynic, the slick politically minded commentator, and the ideologue. So much more vital is the transcendent, a faithfulness to the higher instinct in ourselves and in those around us. There are walks of life where a connection with or a regard for the transcendent is a prerequisite rather than a choice.

Leaving to one side the atheist's rulebook for life and the weary cynicism of the European soul at this moment in history, the underlying themes in the lives of those signed up to our mental health charity are more lucid. Ancient ideas of the demiurge, the creator of this world as read through the texts of Gnosticism, put forward as a symbol if nothing else, might be helpful. The creations of the demiurge are all around us and the suffering of the world is more fully understood and endured with reference to an ignorant creator; or a Jungian analysis of the Old Testament God as developmental and repenting of error by becoming human through the Trinity and sending his son Jesus as Messiah and also as a vindication of his improvement as a creator.

In fields of esoteric study, religion is revisited as poetry, as allegorical morality tales. Secular antipathy towards religion, folk wisdom, and esoteric aspiration betrays an absurd view of human nature, for what tribe or culture on earth came into being without reference to the transcendent? Has such a reductive grouping of people ever existed in the history of humanity? The brand of secularism and atheism often encountered in government departments and publicly funded agencies unites confusion with political correctness, an anti-religious ethos with blind faith in technology and reductive science.

Medical professionals have been disciplined or in some cases removed from their jobs for mentioning religion at the wrong time to the wrong patient. On the wards and in the corridors of the NHS, there is often an anxiety touching on paranoia and silence in all matters to do with religious faith and spiritual succour. In psychiatry the relationship between religious faith and models of recovery is compromised by the often religious nature of mental health delusions and hallucinations. Signs of recovery are measured by the reduction or absence of religiously orientated thoughts and hallucinations. Yet to dissect the religious impulse from the human experience is as ambitious as trying to dissect tenderness, gossip, humour, or an interest in sex from human affairs.

A holistic philosophy of care and support for those with mental health issues must, where necessary. include practical engagement with religious, post-religious, and discarnate ideas. In the spirit of Santayana we can talk about or use aspects of religious thought much as we can talk about and use art, recreation, music, talking therapies, or yoga. The holistic approach falls short, without making gestures to religious impulses and spirituality, as much as this might irritate or frustrate onlookers. Ethereal voices, religious values introduced through the parables of childhood, fearful hallucinations centred on demons and the devil, as well as religious mania, should be engaged with when possible rather than feared and closed down with yet more potent doses of medication or criticism stemming from the materialist philosophy that informs reductive science's growing secularised religion.

When we recategorise such things as belonging to the human imagination, then they become more reasoned. What can be imagined can be reimagined and reinterpreted. There are after all actual recorded happenings linked with other planes outside the human imagination. Somehow the holistic approach must reconcile the damage done by a legion of perverted personalities that infiltrated religious orders with the human need for meaning and commonality of purpose. The damage done is weighed against the mercy of terms big enough to fit as countermeasures against the terrors of what psychiatry describes as hallucinations, but which could equally be described as invisible spiritual parasites, and the reality of the types of dilemmas the mental health worker on the ground must deal with on a daily basis. A genuinely holistic approach presupposes engagement with pseudo-religious and spiritual influences but only when we ourselves have overcome our own preconceptions or have at least recognized what they are. The Mental Health Foundation's report on *The Impact of Spirituality on Mental Health* is succinct in identifying why the implementation of holistic approaches is a problem:

> There are a number of barriers to obtaining an individual's spiritual history, which may need consideration by those working in and planning local and national mental health services. These include:
>
> - a lack of time.
> - a lack of training.
> - concern about stepping outside one's area of expertise.
> - discomfort with the subject.
> - worries about imposing beliefs on the service-user.
> - a lack of interest or awareness.

Potential pitfalls are many but choices on the doorsteps of despair are few. Often it's a question of sticking with it long enough to work out what's really going on and then stretching the vocabulary of engagement or simply dropping the whole idea and running to a saner line of work.

Gareth

Holistic approaches can never be pseudo-theoretical or squeezed out of shape by reductive ideas in biology, evolutionary psychiatry, or textbook social work. If it is only something trendy, part of a politicised programme, something to add to a tick-list, or one of the many games we play, then it is best not to mention it at all. The silence in the eyes of so many with anomalies of mind and spirit cannot be measured using borrowed ideas passed down by research scientists with fixations on laboratory rats, or by categories in psychology research that, much like the Barnum effect, can be applied to nearly everyone at one time or other. It must be a longer game, something real and useful in the world as it stands.

Gareth is one of the guys made for the holistic approach. He filters much of life through art and has closed himself down to other ways of being in the world. He likes early hip-hop and knows every Run DMC lyric in the book. A few years back he went through what he calls a weird few months filled with musical hallucinations, and on certain days he is happy enough to talk about such things. The same tunes went around in his mind on a vivid loop until they became more of a problem than the other hallucinations linked to his diagnosis of bipolar with psychosis.

The three tunes in question were *I Could Be So Lucky* by Kylie Minogue, the theme tune for the TV soap *Coronation Street*, and *What Makes You Beautiful* by One Direction. It sounds grim but Gareth can look back and laugh about it; when all things are considered, musical earworms weren't a big deal in his life and the tunes twirling through his mind didn't last very long. Such intrusions of mind were hardly worth mentioning in the light of how he translates just about everything through the symbolism and colour configurations of art.

A focus on art and how art can help the personality in crisis is useful when working with Gareth. Although he can manage many day-to-day facets of life, he is a fragile guy and is no stranger to the wards of the psychiatric secure wings and hospitals that remain open in this part of London. When he does end up in a mental health hospital, the police are usually involved. Using their sectioning powers, they bring him straight onto the ward, bypassing gate-keeping psychiatric staff who guard mental health beds as if their lives depend on it. When he is psychotic a secure ward with twenty-four-hour staffing and observation is the right place for him to be in. Although it can all become confusing very quickly, our job is to stand shoulder to shoulder with outpatients like Gareth so that hospitalisation and statutory psychiatric intervention are minimised, or become unnecessary. In the absence of much by way of resources the provision of services is at best ad hoc, at worse farcical or tragic. During such uncertain arcs of effort our approaches can become very creative. We become masters of masquerade.

Gareth lives in a house sub-divided into six small living units overlooked by railway arches near St. Thomas' Hospital. Big Ben and the London Eye are backdrops to his medicated days and nights, forever visible through the dusty windows of his small kitchenette. It's a charming, ancient but impersonal corner of the metropolis. Partygoers and an overflow from closing-time pubs use the street just outside the house where Gareth and the others live as a late-night urinal.

Gareth can't take much stimulus, interaction or responsibility if it's not connected to art, computer games or the style of digitalised illustration he finds expression in. His bedroom is full of kit to improve his digital drawings and portraits. He is a skilled illustrator with an art A level, a college diploma in illustration, and the first year of a fine art degree to his name. The work he creates by computer and by hand with charcoal pencils and craft pens is clever, but his personal energy is so low and his concentration so limited that little work is ever done. Like so many signed up to the services of our mental health charity, human potential is subsumed under the numbing cloak of anti-psychotic medicines and the hex of lasting intellectual impairment.

The only effective way of communicating with Gareth is through art, so we focus on the art Gareth has already come up with, deciphering its probable or intended meanings. Once we get to know each other a bit better, we use art as a means through which to connect on a human level. I share the pen and ink drawings I sometimes do at home in my spare time. After a few visits to the men housed near the train archway in Southwark the trust between us grows to where we can talk about things in a little more depth. Sometimes there is even a minute or two to talk about how we might make sense of the roles we find ourselves in.

Gareth isn't ready for spirit work or anything of that nature. It's not that he is uninterested in such things but more about the balance of his mind, more about what he can handle and what he cannot handle. He needs all the reassurance humanly possible, needs as a matter of survival to live in the world of daylight and sunshine rather than in the uncertainty of shadows or in the reality tunnels of people he has never actually met. In psychosis he reports hearing voices, and spirit work to find out more about these voices and then weaken them might help. But he hasn't got to a point in his life where he is ready for any of that. There were moments when he heard me out, listened to how I described voices not as hallucinations but rather as real spiritual entities that are primarily negative. And that the most effective way of limiting their impact is to identity them, isolate them and sap them of their power. The best way to weaken such negative voices is to play up positive voices, though in the process the person in schizophrenia becomes a battle zone for conflicting spiritual entities. With Gareth his positive energies are most associated with art and creativity, so to encourage his art and creative energies is to encourage his best chances of survival and recovery.

The men living in the old Edwardian-era house are just about hanging onto what roughly adds up to a normal life in the community. In the age of the asylum, they would have been institutionalised, their inability to take their roles in society as useful workers acting as unspoken props of shame and inadequacy in a less morally nuanced time. They could not have worked consistently back then as they cannot work consistently now, their minds and constitutions not configured for the usual codes of productivity and the thirty-nine or forty-hour working week. In the days of the asylum, from their inception in the most philanthropic years of the Victorians to the last decades of the twentieth century, the men in the house close to St. Thomas' Hospital would have taken their places among the asylum's population. Unless they had a remarkably kind and committed family, they would have never survived in a pre-welfare state era, or maybe not even in the welfare state at its most resourced.

The house divided into six rooms is by default one of the better examples of community psychiatric care, a top-notch effort by a housing association with a social care division as part of its London catchment area which is not generally known for its success in supporting and housing the mentally ill. The success of the house and the men who live in it is set on simplicity, just as everything to do with the upkeep of the building and what's in place to support the men living there is simple. Every morning a support worker visits the house from their base at a project in nearby Waterloo.

It's a basic welfare check to make sure the men are okay and that any health and safety matters or repairs are reported back to managers, who in turn report to the housing association's maintenance contractors. In a nearby supported housing project managed by the same housing association, support workers visit the old Edwardian house when the men living there need a word or two of advice or practical help with the administration which is the heartbeat of the modern state. From time to time they need support with the paperwork, bleak routines, and medical examinations of the state welfare system.

The men are stable enough for this level of support, with only the occasional relapse and re-route to the nearest mental health ward. Whatever we think about the potential dangers of an anti-psychotic drug like clozapine, it can bring outstanding results when patients' care is well thought-out. Devastating negative symptoms of mental illness can be lessened by clozapine to the point where outpatients can live with a level of independence and a release from the more negative mental health symptoms they could only dream of before. Acute paranoia, thought broadcasting where individuals believe others can read their thoughts, and terrifying voices are ameliorated. Despite the side effects, medication are often the difference between a life worth living and a life where the very question of whether to go on or not hangs morbidly over every waking moment.

Given the challenges of life as we find it and the cipher of chronic mental illness, the care and support for the six men in the shared house is very good. It is basic but effective, especially when we remember where they have come from and how close they are on most days to crisis and hospitalisation. As long as they are reminded now and then to show up on time for their levels testing, the anti-psychotic drug we know as clozapine will go on to remodel their lives, dimming the terrors and anomalies of mind threatening their very sanity, morale, and will to go on.

There is little or no negative energy in the house split into six small living spaces mostly because the men who live there are cared for by a combination of potentially fatal but effective anti-psychotic medication and just about enough practical and moral support from mental health workers. It's good work, an impressive effort of resources and services. Given the imperfection of the human encompassment it's a real victory.

Gareth was brought up by his mother with help from social services as she also suffers from a serious mental health condition. His mother is the only family member he has a relationship with, the one person who would truly grieve if he was successful in one of his sporadic suicide attempts. Lately they have not been talking: the schism between mother and son not straightforward and to do with an alleged insult that, according to the presumed offending party, was actually a compliment.

Researchers at the American Psychological Association analysed data from 2800 participants in a study into the emotional turmoil of unhappy family relationships. They found that significant family relationship strain was linked with a higher incidence of chronic conditions such as stomach trouble and stroke. Psychology tends to have a knack of rewording the obvious, of phrasing in dry terms what most of us already know. In other words, the withdrawal of his mother's love and support is hurting Gareth.

The house divided into six different units and the mental health support workers who call out a few times in any given week are enough to help him hold it all together. Strain from the relationship fallout with his mother is written all over his face and resonates in his every pained word. But for now at least he is holding it together. The wearisome old chestnut of insufficient funding in mental health services wears on him in a less overt way, as he knows nothing about the background squabbles taking place connected with the funding for the services that hold his life together.

It would be nice if he had an allocated social worker or community psychiatric nurse, or if he had a psychiatric review even once a year. The last two reviews they arranged were cancelled at short notice. One of the reviews planned prior to the cancelled reviews didn't happen because the psychiatrist didn't show up. Seemingly the psychiatrist in question, standing in on a short-term basis, was snowed under with work. However, cuts to services and a major deterioration in his relationship with his mother have not landed him back on an acute ward.

Who would have the heart to explain to him that devious cliques of private-sector services have got their claws into public mental health resources, exploiting the growing demand for psychiatric care and intervention? In one quarter of the business year alone, these faceless outfits have claimed £2 billion of NHS funds, taking almost half of the children's and adolescents' budget alone. It is excellent business when we remember it can cost over £700,000 for just one patient for one year's care. An American-based health conglomerate bought the largest private health group in the country for £1.3 billion and now publishes earnings of more than £188 million from our national health service in less than three months.

Another US firm closed 228 deals with the NHS after it bought out a rival group with profits in surplus of £45 million a short time ago. An outfit financed by a private equity firm based in Luxembourg and only in existence for three years is already turning over £61.2 million from over fifty healthcare units. These three firms are responsible for thirteen of the sixteen mental health environments judged inadequate by the Care Quality Commission. Hospitals owned by two of these firms were the subject of troubling undercover television documentaries. One private healthcare group operates eight of the inadequate units criticised by the Care Quality Commission even though its chief executive was given £39 million in one year alone in pay, bonuses, and other benefits.

Greed, cynicism and the kind of corruption so often channelled through the classic business model naturally worms its way into everywhere that a profit can be turned. This would not necessarily be a bad thing if the services in question were adequate and hundreds of millions in taxpayers' money was not redirected into the pockets of already overly-compensated chief executives, senior managers, and shareholders. At UK elections politicians pledge never to undermine or sell off the NHS, when a sizable percentage of it is already compromised by privatisation, or completely sold off with the inevitable trashing of workers' rights. It is an incorrect use of public funds that diminishes the quality of services and which is widely tolerated.

Gareth accepts the continual fall-off of care and support as he has no choice. Care and support workers must reach yet deeper inside themselves to compensate for cuts and shrinking resources which are now more readily redirected into the bank accounts of private-sector bosses and overseas' shareholders. The men in the house divided into six separate parts must accept whatever care and support they are offered, as they are not assertive in any way and do all they can to keep clear of stress and confrontation.

Yet for all the graft and shifting of resources from frontline services to dodgy pockets in the private sector, the house near St. Thomas' hospital where Gareth is accommodated and supported is almost a paradigm of good care. How much of this is incidental is hard to say but in simple terms it is a good place to visit, and to live in. People are genuinely cared for here and the negative symptoms of the often-devastating condition we know as schizophrenia are met head-on by a purposeful recipe of clozapine, decent accommodation, and regular but not intrusive input from support workers.

In his living space Gareth is relaxed and willing to talk, now used to the tick-list. Once the bare minimum of red tape is out of the way we can talk about art, since it's only art that resonates with him. In many parts of the world or throughout most of what we understand as history, none of this would happen. There would be no publicly-funded accommodation complete with electricity, a fire-alarm system, solid door locks to keep intruders out, a twenty-four hour heating system, and visiting support workers with big hearts. The best the men could hope for in the past was the asylum dorm, enough to eat, and not too much by way of rough handling from the asylum attendants. In so many regions of the world they would expect nothing, only what they might forage for in public bins. They might find themselves chained to a post by a relative and fed on scraps, and belittled for their lack of productivity and for the trouble they brought to their families. Or, as we might expect there would be the charitable institution or shelter reeking of defeat and unhappiness, a bed of perpetual discomfort in someone else's house.

Here, almost in the shadow of St. Thomas' Hospital, this house, with its six sensitive souls so often haunted by how they experience the world of the senses, is a truly humane intervention. It means a lot. It's a lot more than a house where six mental health outpatients live.

It's a flag of hope for a troubled species. It's a triumph as meaningful as the Olympic Flame or a sunrise on a beautiful morning.

With so much already in place we can now use holism to honour Gareth's individual take on the world around him. He has drawn a funny image of an animal-like face wearing some kind of hat. He's colourised it on his computer and it stands out as a funny if distorted cartoon.

What is it?

It's a policewoman.

It's a bit disturbing (*I say looking at it more closely*). Is this how you see the police?

Yeah. You could say that.

When Gareth gets sectioned it's always the police who get the job of handcuffing him and bundling him into the back of an ambulance or police wagon. These experiences have shaped his slant on what the police look like. It's a sneering spectre, much like how the policewoman it is based on must have appeared to Gareth at the time when he was last sectioned. It's the artwork he's most proud of.

There is not much artwork to talk about as he just does not have the energy, psychic or otherwise, to create anything at all on a consistent basis. So we talk about the handful of illustrations he managed to do in recent years, usually just before a mental health relapse when his spurts of energy can backflip into mania. We also talk about new work that he is planning, and when we talk about new work his eyes light up. He has so many ideas about art he would like to talk about, but there is so much left unsaid.

We talk about art in the section of the old house allocated to Gareth, a kind of maisonette with damp walls and small clusters of what look like fungus growing from the corners of the ceiling. So many of South London's old buildings are cradled in damp and rot. His floor is unswept, his living space cluttered with disassembled computer parts and assorted junk. He is perhaps as contented here as he could be anywhere else, given his mental health susceptibilities and the sensitivity of his very being. There is a fair likelihood that there will be more mental health sections in the future, with an ambulance parked outside the old Edwardian house in the shadows of St. Thomas' Hospital—a symbol of a civilisation's answer to the howling rage of a troubled man.

Questions to do with other kinds of consciousness or healing rituals of the arcane are not needed here. The creeping dominance of scientism and scepticism in so many realms of life and over so many years has downgraded the shamanism of other cultures and moves on into yet darker spheres where it leaves behind both secular prophets and free-thinkers. He has internalised much of the bogus information that's out there and to mention such things would bring up much fear planted over time by aberrations in our culture. Only art makes sense here. Talk of art gets through to him. He gets it, understands the prompts to do with everyday tasks once they are couched in terms of art. We talk about exhibitions in the big galleries and about his limited number of artworks, the illustrations often processed through graphic designing software.

The holistic approach is at its most simple here, balancing on the back of a beautifully reductive mix of anti-psychotic medication and support from a large housing association more known for their indifference and occasional callousness towards their support workers and dislike of basic employment rights, as much as for their caring deficits. But here they have got it right. And consolidating how they have got it right with a simplified holistic approach set dead in the centre of Gareth's art is probably as good as it's going to get. This is not the time or place for spirit work to tease out the positive and isolate the spiritual parasites at the apex of so much of Gareth's suffering. But on another day's march, it might be the right time and place.

Gareth's Impression of a Bed-Bug

Gareth's Drawing of the "Perfect Domestic Pet"

Gareth's Impression of the "Typical Person"

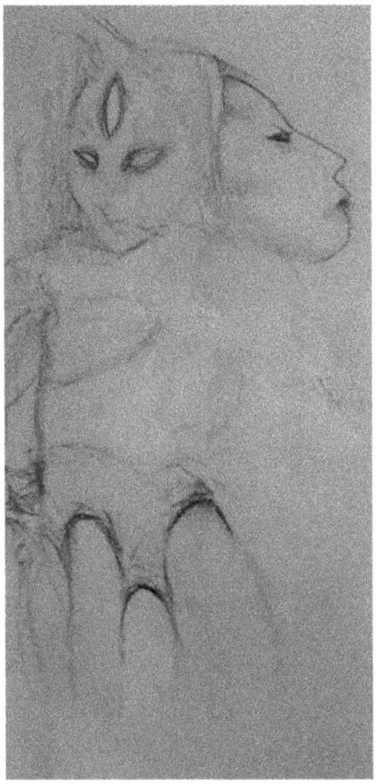

Gareth's Drawing of "The Perfect Woman"

Gareth's Painting of a Policewoman

Kenny

Most of the time things work on the principle of expediency. Often at the last minute in a rush of anxiety what needs to be done is done. Emergency laws are brought in during viruses, rioting, terror attacks, and other threats to the status quo. Money, landlordism, the institutions of state and governance, the property principle, and a series of important treaties and international agreements are protected as a priority. The population is deceived if it believes that the central authority has any abiding interest in their welfare. It doesn't. Why would it? It is a beast of necessity surviving in a chaotic world.

Citizens are often confused when they ring the police at three in the morning to report that the walls of their bedroom are literally vibrating because of their neighbour's loud party music. They are told it is not a police matter and given the number of a council environmental health contact. If they manage to get through to anyone, there will be another futile conversation and parting words of advice to contact the council during working hours. Bleary-eyed from sleeplessness they will show up at their job the next morning feeling just a little more demoralised and unsure about their place in a society that can often appear to be an enemy. For those with the time and money, there is the law and many do dedicate chunks of their time and resources trying to use the law to iron out some facet or other of daily living that in a more functional and civilised part of society is already ironed out.

We masquerade as functional citizens in a dysfunctional society, alienated by an accelerating version of radical consumerism that has stripped so much mythos and sense of community from the culture we are part of. We can easily find ourselves at the baseline of sanity while we console ourselves that at least it's better than wars of unimaginable destruction. That is the context in which we masquerade as mental health workers who are meant to have answers to questions put to us by men and women with voices booming in their minds and with personalities from outside their minds mocking them. We must respond in a way that is in keeping with the zeitgeist of the moment. We parrot the wisdom of the age that categorises such voices and personalities as hallucinations. We hand on what we know about psychotropic medication and its side-effects.

In our roles we prop up the way things are in the country's administration and treatment of the mentally ill. Good and evil, right and wrong have little if anything to do with it. If we must collude in the long-term poisoning through medication of individuals with enduring psychiatric diagnoses, then that is what we do. Moral points or reasoning may be tagged onto our work, but it can only ever help to convince the rational part of us that we have a sense of moral agency in what we are doing. We are required to support the mentally ill within the framework of a treatment model based on continuous and often very high doses of psychotropic medication. We address the side-effects of medication with guidelines from prescribing agencies, the NHS, supervising mental health nurses and psychiatrists, and of course the psychopharmacology industry.

In this model the voices experienced by the mentally ill are auditory hallucinations, and side-effects such as heavy, persistent sedation are unavoidable burdens to be endured. To go beyond this model, we must masquerade as outriders of psychopharmacology and operate in the shadows. The observer might well ask why. Why put ourselves through this frustrating ordeal day after day in roles that pay badly and where exploitation and harassment from managers are to be expected? The natural answer to this question lies in the voices and personalities experienced by those in psychosis and in paranoid schizophrenia. If such voices and personalities originate in another realm of being, be it the Jungian concept of the collective unconscious or the Astral Plane, then an equal font of inspiration must be a factor to some extent or other in the actions of those who take on the mental health roles in question.

Something beyond our conscious thoughts compels us to take on this fight, as much as something beyond the conscious thoughts of the mentally disordered we care for is the source of their malaise and torment. The contest takes place on a higher level than the few cubic centimetres on which our rationality is said to be centred.

On a more practical level, getting to Kenny's block of council flats is not what you would call convenient. The most useful bus passes about a mile away from his front door and then it's a hike through the peripheries of an unwelcoming and drab South London housing estate. Concrete gable-ends tagged in a hip hop scheme of colour mutely ask the only questions worth asking. Are we really meant to live like this? What is really going on? Just where does the concrete end and the human soul begin?

Locals wait at bus stop shelters and pass in and out of granite tunnels and glum walkways wearing what can appear as masks of psychic pain. Many are vivacious souls weaned under sunny postcolonial skies and now downcast under layers of clothing, faced with a landscape stripped of ritual and kinship bonds. Innocuous words and gestures are easily misunderstood here. There's uneasiness in the air and it's hard to ignore this. The lifts in Kenny's block are out of order, and on the way up a dismal claustrophobic stairway a twitchy guy with sunken cheeks jogs past on his way down. His eyes are alarmed and dilated, and he scratches so forcefully at his bare arms that he leaves long red marks on his skin.

Kenny is very unhappy. His unhappiness manifests in waves of negative vibes forceful enough to stifle the energy of anyone who hangs out with him for even a few minutes. He is angry too, so angry his hands often tremble. Spittle flies from his lips in unforeseen directions when he speaks. His flat is filthy. In a saner world the flat would be condemned and an order served from environmental health to clean it up under threat of eviction. But the policy of independent living in the community is an article of faith for so many senior managers, commissioners and bureaucrats who order the lives of the consistently poor. To get someone like Kenny to do something he doesn't feel like doing is not as linear as it might first appear.

On my last visit he complained about another mental health outpatient who defecates in the lifts. I ask if the council or the police know about it. He said yes, they know all about it. And what have they done about it? It seemed like a rational question to ask. Nothing. They have done nothing. Kenny is adamant. His hands are trembling again and he is staring at me with a world of hurt in his eyes. Seemingly the guy who uses the lift as a toilet is trying to get readmitted to the local psychiatric hospital. The ex-patient is certain that if he racks up enough antisocial behaviour points they will send him there. So far he's got nowhere with it.

Kenny wants to go back to hospital too, even though he swears that his last admission was without exception the worse time of his life. What is this malaise gnawing away at the human soul, gnawing and snapping until the very breath of life itself becomes a hated enemy? What can any of us offer or say to Kenny to ease whatever suffering is haunting his days and nights? Is it about expectation? In Kenny's growing years he'd have been drilled in the expectations of the age, coached like generations were coached in the philosophy of material gain increasing for all. And in material gain all the yearnings of the heart are promised to be satisfied. The message of hope extends to all parts of life and to practically everyone, spreading in a gigantic bubble of illusion. It was never about accepting the tragedy and limitations of life for ordinary people and finding joy in what is joyful, but rather about new ways of perpetuating the hope that the poor can one day live like the rich. When we spend a lifetime looking in a specific direction, we are naturally surprised when hit by a speeding train coming from the other direction.

Though born and raised in South London he has never heard of an earlier South Londoner William Blake, but when I mention Blake's work *Songs of Innocence and Experience* he says it rings a bell. English schools included Blake's earlier poems in their curriculums but not the longer, prophetic works. Blake's god of reason in *The Book of Urizen* explains how the mind is held prisoner on earth and is robbed of eternity and light. It can seem as if arcane knowledge of the past is so often like a family secret nobody wants to mention, an infanticide where the family's most promising infant is served up to the demigods of ignorance for fear that they might grow into a shining paradigm and embarrass everyone with higher standards.

Kenny has insight into his illness. He hears voices, most of them negative, and understands that the anti-psychotic medication he is taking weaken the impact of the voices. The disembodied whispers that remain are mostly neutral or benign. He has never found alcohol in any way interesting or worthwhile and can't remember the last time he had a beer or a wine. Last Christmas? Maybe the Christmas before? Drugs were his thing and he used drugs with a fearless heart in his late teens and twenties. That is where it went wrong. It is Kenny's abiding belief that he warped his mind by taking too many drugs, physically tearing crucial layers of membrane in his brain and damaging the pineal gland.

> People like me are damaged. We done harm to ourselves with drugs. We'll never get better.

Kenny is not self-pitying when he speaks. His tone is flat, as flat and dispassionate as when people state a basic fact of their life. I was married once but now I'm divorced. Once I wrote poetry in my spare time. Once I liked fly-fishing. I damaged my brain with drugs and I don't expect to be normal again. After ringing the bell, I wait longer than usual at the door to Kenny's flat. When he finally opens the door, his features are stiff from a stubborn, devastating depression which is as much a part of him as the loose NHS spectacles dangling crookedly across the bridge of his nose. Barely acknowledging the presence of a visitor, just a nod and a grunt, and the most perfunctory look of indifference, he turns numbly away, dragging his body back into the dark interior of the flat.

He is one of the new generation of mental health fire-starters, setting fire to a plastic sink unit in a mental health hostel a few years back. It was enough to have him sent to prison. It seems out of proportion, I said at one of the first meetings we had. To be prosecuted for setting fire to a plastic sink in a mental health hostel? Could the staff not have dealt with it? Did they have to call the police?

> They hate us mate. They pretend to like us but that's all bollocks. We mean nothing to them. Nothing. They make a wage out of us and control us so as the government can say it's doing its duty to the mentally ill. But really they hate us. If they could they'd shove us all in a gas chamber. But then they'd have to find another way of paying their mortgages. So on second thoughts they wouldn't want to do that. But they hate us. So there's no way they're going to give a toss about us. If they could they've have set me on fire.

Kenny's hands are now shaking as he speaks. Small, slight and stooped, there's a week's grey stubble on his jowls and he looks even smaller as he rants against those who personify the system, which he is certain oppresses him. Standing by a living-room wall with spiralling patterns of dirt engrained in it and with his hands shaking, there is something unusually honest about him, as if it would literally kill him to misrepresent the reality he is faced with, or to involve himself in any way with lies, deceit, or the phoniness of a world he remains at a distance from. His truthfulness and integrity are outraged by the circumstances of his life as much as by the powerlessness, which binds him to relative poverty in a wealthy land.

Throughout our urban spaces a defeated legion of damaged souls cling to life in parallel conditions—mental health fire-starters forced to live in flats without support or meaning in their lives, living on a vague promise that one day something referred to as "progress" in its broader sense will save them. When in crisis they torch their flats. They are then routed through the criminal justice system and can be found in the old Victorian-era prisons of London and as well as the smaller prisons. They rock to and fro like traumatised bomb-blast victims, laughing manically when they see themselves in security mirrors, as if seeing themselves for the very first time.

The condition of many of the flats and maisonettes defies description. Filth, faeces, and urine are testimonies to a caring deficit, yet more signs perhaps of some darker age to come. Somehow the isolation of individuals, the erosion of social bonds, and the failure of the experiment to close down hospitals and institutions and decant a population of the sick and needy into a mythical community, has snowballed into a circus of neglect and the passing of blame onto somewhere or someone else. In place of intervention, structure, a daily programme, and ongoing assessments, there are often only remnants of a fragmenting and far more censorious welfare system. We wait for the mentally ill to implode, and when they do, they will for the most part be hurried through the normal statutory routes.

We find them in the corridors of accident and emergency annexes with bloodied bandages around their wrists, in the holding cells of magistrates' courts, in police cells, in prisons, and in the psychiatric wards that remain. NHS commissioners and psychiatrists, community psychiatric nurses, and mental health trust managers pretend there's a coherent and humane system when everybody on the ground knows there isn't. The system stopped working a long time ago. Now nobody even pretends to know how to reset it. People on extraordinarily high salaries keep alive an illusion of a humane system, sacrificing ideals of professional integrity, duty of care, and conscience to the beastly needs of the human ego and the earthly stomach. If this analysis of the psychiatric hierarchy seems harsh or unfair, please bear in mind it is more an analysis of perception and experience rather than an analysis of selective data, academic findings and press releases.

Existentialist methods in therapy are in part a synthesis of the will of the optimist and are focussed against the presenting powerlessness of those in crisis. They shift the language of custom through the means of expression. Thus "it hurts" is transformed into the more personalised "I hurt". And from there it is a shorter leap of language to further transform "they are hurting me" into "I am hurting myself by how I interpret their behaviour". It is a subtle sidestep of expression, a metamorphosis from victim to a self-authorising mental state, where there is more awareness of what is happening. Through the re-evaluation of language, we can move towards a more expressively neutral zone, in theory at least.

In his book *Quantum Psychology*, Robert Anton Wilson's E-Prime reconfigurations of simple sentences are practical while at the same time radical. "John is unhappy and grouchy" is e-primed as "John appears unhappy and grouchy in the office". And "the photon is a wave" e-primes as "the photon behaves as a wave when constrained by certain instruments".

Everyday perceptions of madness reduce the subject to a spiritual and psychic state of impotence where language games are useless, even language games as clever as those of Robert Anton Wilson. In madness there is nowhere to run with the natural inclinations of the human will and its biological determinants. In madness an initial obfuscation of mind is compounded by rage or confusion or disorientation at the loss of social credibility, potential to work and earn, and the impositions of psycho-pharmaceutical medication. Standing language up on its head does not really help. Here's how Kenny outlines this sense of helplessness and lack of will:

> You have a freedom pass so you can travel on the buses all day if you like. And that's what you do. Go around on the buses all day with no money in your pockets. You'd love to kill yourself but haven't got the balls to do it.

In urban spaces the misery is intensified by the impersonality of what passes as social interaction. Cuts to welfare and provision of care introduced in the austerity years of the post-Lehmann Brothers collapse notched up the pressure. The mentally ill woke to a new regime of increased state intrusion and re-evaluation. An era dawned of disquieting ATOS medical assessments and the deduction of social security payments for nominal infringements, often resulting in zero income for weeks or months.

On the tail of this new regime was a campaign to demonise the poor which rallied almost every media outlet in the land to its cause. Suicides increased and the NHS was besieged by record numbers frantic for emergency help. The chief executive of the NHS pointed out that he had predicted such a meltdown when the extent of the cuts to social care was announced. It hardly takes a genius of human observation to know that, when the sick and mentally disordered are not cared for at home, or at what passes as home, they will sooner or later need hospitalisation. The cuts to services affect the mentally ill as much as any analogous social group, but surprisingly Kenny is not unduly worried by them.

He has stepped back to the very limit where the smallest backward movement will then tip him into a chasm of spiritual or physical death. He stops short of taking his own life or becoming homeless on the streets, because he understands that homelessness in a British winter is akin to death, or will at the very least quicken death. Kenny understands that he really ought to be cared for in an institution or at least in a housing scheme of some type, which takes into account his limitations. But owing to the convolutions of a highly taxed and wealthy society never really at ease with itself, and indifferent turns of fate, he finds himself living in a council flat with the visits of a mental health charity worker to help him through the workings of his own thoughts. I ask Kenny about the professionals who had supported him through his mental health crises, and his eyes are rivets of remembered suffering as he answers:

> They don't care about us, mate. One or two are all right but most of them are outright bastards. I've had a psychiatrist laugh into my face once. There I was sitting in front of him in tears and he just laughed in my face. I hate all of them. They just dope us up and patronise us.

Again, we might ask what is this unhappiness infesting entire populations like a plague? It is vivid in Kenny, part of his primary energy as a person in the world. There is now a real effort in mental health practice to avoid blanket categorisations as they can dehumanise. Categorisation locates people in boxes, whether it sets out to or not. And boxes are not the best beginning for the creative unravelling of the dysfunctional narrative.

Kenny and so many others have their wills weakened by involvement with mental health charities and community psychiatric teams. There is reluctance from anyone involved in their care to dare mention the usual motivational ideas so central to the talking therapies pioneered by Freud and his followers. They are judged to need a more direct and practical intervention. Subsequently you will find them bending over at a given day every month to take the jabbed cocktail of anti-psychotic drugs known as the depot injection. Or they will hold out palmate hands every evening for pills to be tapped out from a dosette box. Or they are selected from the general population of our prisons and escorted to Broadmoor, Ashworth, or Rampton high security hospitals. Or they are monitored closely by staff in mental health hostels or lie medicated in psychiatric wards on suicide watch.

Kenny's dependency on state psychiatry is compounded by a low-spirited dependency on the state. He has been in the system for so long he's lost whatever skills he had to enable him to live independently of the psychiatrists, pharmacists, and community mental health nurses he so despises. He has thought it over, pondered it into the witching hours of many long nights, and talked about it with everyone he has met in the mental health system who showed even the slightest interest.

The pressure on the person who suffers from mental disorder can in certain circumstances compel them to do or say almost anything. In so many ways Kenny is no different to you or me. He is obliged to stick to the rules of society and laws of the land whether he likes it or not. His main issue is more about powerlessness, his mental and emotional problems aggravated by a failure over decades to deal with the problems in his life and to find any kind of self-reliance. Maybe he just didn't fight hard enough against a system which medicated him into the kind of passivity hierarchical systems prefer. Often Kenny's sense of helplessness in the face of what he sees as hopeless odds echoes a deeper wisdom from the origins of our civilisation.

> He lays the sins of the parents upon the children; the entire family is affected—even children in the third and fourth generations.
>
> (Numbers 14:14)

The profundity of what ails him calls to the highest notions of human yearning. A crippling dysfunction centred in the dynamics of his family of origin could very well be at play. Later in *Numbers* we are reminded of the psychological shadow that falls on those guilty through a tribal or family connection to a crime, error or act of defiance:

> And your children will be like shepherds, wandering in the wilderness for forty years.

I hope this not the case for Kenny, and that he is not jinxed by an ancient curse that is rephrased in today's therapy spaces as enmeshment. Forty years, after all, is a very long time in one life.

The psychiatric hierarchy has a societal role to play and its very survival pivots on how well it plays this role. Medicating and weakening Kenny's spirit and force of personality through interventions is not a moral worry for them. Kenny opened himself to the power of other wills to the point that it was almost certain that the psychiatric system or the will of a more forceful person would dominate him. Over the years Kenny has sleepwalked further and yet further down a path to more powerlessness and dependency on people he mostly hates. The psychiatric system promotes and protects its own power and privileges over all else, much like any organisation or hierarchy, in a world often more cynical than we are led to believe. If people like Kenny feel they have literally lost their souls and integrity, then so be it. The more innocent among us make the mistake of believing that the psychiatric protocols in place are first and foremost intended to cure the mentally disordered. The reality is far more nuanced.

Naturopathic doctors like Peter Glidden are now referenced more in the treatment of cancer. Dr. Glidden has this to say on the power of medical orthodoxy:

> The only reason chemotherapy is used is because doctors make money from it—period. It doesn't work 97% of the time. If Ford Motor Company made an automobile that exploded 97% of the time would they still be in business? No.

Another naturopathic doctor Leonard Coldwell is critical of the template of the modern medical doctor, which is their training:

> The problem is the way doctors are trained. No medical doctor ever learns about curing anything. They learn about chemical intervention or surgery to suppress symptoms. They don't go for the root cause.

Coldwell goes onto speak about the high rates of suicide and drug and alcohol abuse among doctors:

> These guys figure out over time that they have no tools and that they are murdering and have murdered their patients. You go into the medical profession, the first year, the first two years, you're really excited, you're really into it, you're giving your all, until you find out that no matter what you do the patient gets worse, or they cure themselves. These poor doctors figure out they cannot help. The medical profession is a religion.

The psychiatrists who have so much power in his life are neither Kenny's friends, nor his social peers. What can he actually expect from them? He's fallen into a trap of dependency and is not on a dissimilar wavelength to the naturopaths Glidden and Coldwell in that he knows there's something seriously wrong with the medical and psychopharmacological prudence handed down from on-high, knows there is a lot more going on than what he has been told. A thousand causal factors stretching back in a thousand different directions have brought him here to a medical and psychiatric system manipulated by the pharmaceutical industry. Much like the cancer doctor is allowed to only use chemotherapy, surgery, and radiotherapy with cancer diagnoses, the psychiatrist is only allowed to use rudimentary talking-therapies and pharmaceutical drugs in treating mental disorder.

Kenny's only real hope of freeing himself from dependence is to tune into the powers of his own psyche. If he can get used to looking for answers in his own consciousness and impulses at the base of his consciousness, then this in itself is a step away from psychiatric-assisted helplessness. For example, a simple ritual can act as an exercise of self-will in action. It can change the emphasis from outer to inner, from dependency on others to notions of the transcendent.

In deference to humanist psychology the men and women in question have not yet journeyed from the baseline of Maslow's pyramid to be ready for any kind of talking therapy. These are pretty desperate cases, casualties of damaged families; the hyper-consumerist society with all its unnatural adaptations and winners and losers; a self-inflicted cure by whatever hedonism can be found at the modern crossroads; organic brain damage; low I.Q; chronic poverty of the soul; genetic mutation; or a combination of all these factors and others. If they were of value or interest to society or protected by persons or institutions with status, they wouldn't allow our mental health charity anywhere near them.

A common factor in the lives of the men and women in the care of mental health charities is their poverty. Invariably they did not exactly sparkle before psychiatric involvement. They were more often unemployed or employed in low-paying dead-end jobs. Typically, their dysfunction is so grounded in family dynamics, socio-genetic conditioning, and educational under-performance that it is impossible to see where their socialisation ends and their personality begins. They are not the high achievers who have imploded in the middle of a professional career or a worthwhile project. They are poor and uninteresting by society's median evaluation and by the ethics of the day.

Causal factors in their decline are as much a part of social history and economic conditions as a part of a psychopathological theory. They cannot play a part financially in a rehab programme or private therapy, or afford a break far away from the social conditions which are such a primary causal factor in their crisis. In an earlier century they would have looked for help from cunning-folk or from the healing wells and simples of the old faith. Now they have psychopharmacology, interventions from impersonal state agencies, and a hyper-consumerism they can only hope to take part in in their best hours.

On visits to Kenny my mind scans inner tapes of reference, scavenging the odd idea or memory from readings in existentialism and the arcane. Always hoping not to say the wrong thing, I regurgitate the occasional analogy or quirky story from the day's news. It can help to share the funniest jokes that come to mind, as they are a reminder that we are all human. But what proves most helpful is an interest in the arcane. In our conversations with Kenny, I mention different ways of looking at any given situation in the hope of opening up the pathways of human communication wide enough so that we can both speak freely.

I speak about art and its importance for guys like Gareth, but he's unmoved. For the most part he is barely interested or is guarded and his answers are monosyllabic. Only what concerns him right away brings more than a grunt or a nod. His bluntness is not unexpected.

Out here in these fields of misunderstanding it is fairly normal and understandable. Niceties of everyday conversation are elbowed to one side. With the mentally disordered every word is a potential landmine. No matter how innocent, every word is judged and weighed for authenticity, measured for potential weakness and insincerity. The kind of chatter overheard at the office watercooler or coffee-point is quickly misconstrued when echoed in the rehabilitation spaces of the mentally disordered. When silence is golden then words must slip like liquid silver from our lips.

I didn't bring it up but must have mentioned it at some time or other. He stopped what he was doing and looked at me with a whole new world of curiosity in his eyes. He never wanted to get very much into talking about drugs, but he said enough for me to guess he'd had plenty of hallucinogenic trips before it all went so badly wrong. It is not surprising. Pink Panther tabs on the Magic Bus to the 'Dam, parties stretching into garbled days and nights, and dry-mouthed comedowns courtesy of the wicked wonders of amphetamine sulphate. Everyone was young once. A social commentator wrote about the years 1975 to 2000 and described them as the defining years of the New Age we hear so much about. In this inspired age so much had changed, and Kenny's maturation into early manhood happened in the New Age. He has danced through the Acid House revolution and was so liberal with drugs he has probably damaged his brain for good. Just what exactly he has seen on his less inhibited nights he is not saying.

He is curious about the arcane and asks me what I know about it. Any two-way conversation is a victory in itself as he has never asked me a single question about my life before and showed no interest whatsoever in my existence as a fellow human being. As far as he's concerned I'm just another disposable foot-soldier in servitude to the convention of the day, another interchangeable pawn of a hated social construction, much like he sees himself as a pawn of a hated social construction. This time in the space of a few short sentences he is interested in what I have to say and has actually shaken himself out of his usual torpor long enough to ask me a question which is not cynical or draped in self-destruction, rage, self-pity, or deep depression.

There's another question to follow. We both sense it must be asked as we go through the humdrum support work, which keeps him part of the system he hates so much. We run through a questionnaire and a short tick-sheet for the local authority, and he signs them without taking any notice of what they are. I explain what they are and their importance in relation to his tenancy but he is not listening. His awareness of personal responsibility has long since faded. He stopped caring a long time ago. Statistically he should be dead anyway, but motorcycle accidents, a collapsed lung, drug overdoses, suicide attempts, and a baseball bat clubbing from a drug dealer which fractured his skull haven't killed him. As I run through the routine paperwork, the question squats between us. He knows what it is and I know what it is. The only real certainty is not why there is a question unasked between us, but just how he's is going to word it.

As I'm about to leave, he tells me about a dream he keeps having. In the dream his flat detaches itself from the block it is part of and travels at a blinding speed into deep space. It is sucked into a vortex leading to a totally dissimilar world. He says the dimensions, landscapes and colours of this outlandish world are beyond description. Only after the briefest few seconds in this wondrous scene his flat spins back to earth and he wakes up in his bed. He had his medication changed only the week before by a new psychiatrist and he wonders if this might be the reason behind the dream.

Astrophysicists have identified a massive black hole in the middle of the Milky Way, which they believe might be a doorway to other galaxies. It is a black hole of unimaginable vastness where space and time are transmuted outside the boundaries of scientific knowledge. Maybe the dream is related to this black hole. Maybe somewhere in the outer fields of knowledge the idea of the astrophysicists' doorway to other worlds found its way into Kenny's dreamlife. Is it impossible? He finds this intriguing and wants to talk about it, but I am already running late. There will be other days when we can talk about it but for now the hands of time dictate that I must keep moving.

I am almost out the door when he asks the question I know he's been longing to ask. It's a simple question. He wants to know if I think the arcane can help him, his voice now more agreeable and with the usual anger almost not present. He is close to childlike as he waits by the door for an answer. There's a trace of hope on his face that I haven't seen before. I answer in the affirmative. Sure, I say. I think the wisdom of the arcane can help. A holistic approach is open to all reasonable questions and the arcane is reasonable. Everything else seems to have failed for him.

His boredom and lack of engagement with the world are further barriers to recovery. John Watkins' words from his holistic study *Living with Schizophrenia* are helpful:

> Much of a patient's action of self-abuse or transgressions against others may stem from a painful "boredom". In a recent study, when patients recovering from psychosis in the community were interviewed about their lives, "their principle complaint was of boredom—rated by them as much more problematic than psychotic symptoms", and the high prevalence of their using stimulants and mind-altering drugs and sleeping excessively is a consequence of what they feel to be empty and uninteresting lives.

I check my watch. It really is time to go. As I hurry away to the next appointment Kenny steps into the hallway. I glance at his expression in parting and see yet more hope in the stubble and broken bones now healed into a lesser arrangement of a human face.

Peter

Something changed. There was hope on Kenny's face as he watched me leave. It didn't come across as just another phantom hope. Psychiatric and social care systems so often default to a kind of minimalism which just about satisfies the legislation in place. Many social care managers and senior caseworkers must have taken a second look at their old risk assessments when they came across Kenny again, amazed he is still alive. He has gone through the system numerous times, and injury, age, and medication have slowed him up, yet here he is. He has had a thousand conversations with a thousand mental health and social care professionals. But the fundamental malaise of his life is pretty much unchanged. His misery and unhappiness are there for all to see, his anger and raging fits deep-seated parts of his character. Isolated, weakened by medication, and state dependent, he cannot begin to understand the overall calamity of his life.

In the absence of a mythology to honour him as a channel for voices from other planes, his fantastical descriptions of what he sees and hears are muted and waved away as the pointless ravings of a sick mind. In the heights of mania his skewed logic, euphoria, or terrors were recorded by psychiatric ward staff, who for the most part listened politely inside their time-limits. They then ticked off the dishevelled words as belonging to the categories and sub-categories of madness. These experiences are quickly swallowed in a simplified ideology of hyper-consumerism and competitiveness, which swallows all the waking seconds and minutes. As the old saying goes, time is money. In the logic of our times only another madman would sit listening and recording the delusions of a madman.

From Plotinus to Carl Jung and Henri Bergson there is a reliable school of thought predicating the idea of consciousness as animate not only in mental states but outside mental states too. If human consciousness can locate manifestations of energy autonomous from the physical entity we know as the brain, then what questions do these expressions present to clinicians faced with auditory and visual hallucinations?

If the reasoning of Jung and Bergson is broadened, then at the very least there is a doubt as to whether consciousness is something that only happens within minds. Such a doubt is a problem for the mental health professional recording the words of patients who see, hear, and sense things outside the usual human spectrum of sensual experience. Instead of categorising the fantastical descriptions as delusional and psychotic, a more holistic application of thought would be to pencil a question mark after each vague comment or narrative. After all, in the wider view the likelihood exists of a source of consciousness not centred in the human mind, communicating in some way with the person voicing a disjointed narrative.

Several Eastern philosophical viewpoints are panpsychic in nature, and in synch in a number of ways with western psychophysical or non-dualist points of view. In panpsychism the idea of consciousness centred outside the human mind is condensed into a view where all things have a mind or mind-like quality. From Thales to Spinoza and Leibniz, from Schopenhauer to Bergson, panpsychism is part of an argument that sits apart from the materialist model of consciousness as something that only happens in the mind.

For Bergson the brain does not bring consciousness into being, but is rather part of consciousness. Bergson's veracity of thought is in part brought into the open by those who criticised him. French professors accused him of spiritualism, the Vatican accused him of pantheism, and he was criticized in Bertrand Russell's eccentric tome *The History of Western Philosophy*. Such criticism reshapes itself through time and can now be considered an endorsement. This philosophical point, when added to the hearing of voices often linked with mental illnesses such as schizophrenia, brings yet another question mark regarding the structure of such voices. It takes us nearer to the idea of a consciousness situated outside the human psyche as a discarnate starting place from where sounds are transmogrified and then perceived by a few sensitive minds among us.

A holistic view of consciousness as existing outside the human mind is recorded by Ingrid Elfferich in her contribution to Prof. Marius Romme's seminal work *Accepting Voices*:

> … there may be planes and dimensions surrounding and interpenetrating our physical lives, influencing us in ways which are not yet fully understood. This metaphysical view suggests that, on some level of our consciousness, we are interconnected not only with the living but also with the dead, who may still exist in another dimension of reality such as some clairvoyants claim to be able to perceive.

An idea of consciousness as centred not in the physical brain is most capably elucidated by Rupert Sheldrake, the British scientist and parapsychologist. Sheldrake's conclusions based on thorough research over many years have weighty inferences for our understanding of consciousness. After reading Sheldrake and then listening to someone talking about their auditory hallucinations, a natural question to ask is "where exactly are the voices coming from?" Hard materialist perspectives lifted from experimental laboratories and mathematical deductions are applied unapologetically to spheres of life outside the scientist's remit. Cosmologists posit theories of dark matter, dark energy, and multiverses without plausible corroboration. We just have to believe: much as medieval Europeans were obliged to believe the Vatican regardless of how counter-intuitive Papal Bulls and decrees seemed.

One consequence of the hard materialist line propped up by so many educationalists, most scientists, and nearly all the media, is to strip the Western soul of holistic truth and mystery and to cap the Western mind so that it functions in error much like a tragic fabrication of an ignorant demiurge. It insists on a robotic worldview which it then projects out into the cosmos. It infiltrates what it sees as the educated mind, because those educated in the usual way are expected to share in the stark materialist point of view, at least in public.

A certain defeatism largely brought on by this odd march through the decades by this school of materialism could be heard in the gloomy prognosis of the GP I tried to discuss Tina's case with before visiting her. It drapes itself like an immense wet blanket over all our work with the poor, mentally disordered, and addicted. It predicts the worse and, as it sees humanity as little more than mechanistic, tends to expect the worse. There is no scope for other views of consciousness, much less for miracles. West African shaman Malidoma Patrice Somé is prominent in a culture where mental illness is the sign of a healer. In the world of the African shaman, mental disorders are spiritual crises, occurrences where healers are chosen by a consciousness not located in the human mind. This is what Shaman Somé had to say after visiting an American psychiatric hospital:

> I was so shocked. This was the first time I was brought face to face with what is done to people exhibiting the same symptoms I've seen in my village. So this is how the healers who are attempting to be born are treated. What a loss! What a loss that a person who is finally being aligned with a power from the other world is just being wasted.

What we know as schizophrenia, psychosis, schizoid-affective disorder, and similar disorders of the mind may be a climatic modification of the psyche. Shaman Somé goes on to say that what we in the west regard as mental illness the Dagara tribe of Burkina Faso and Ghana understand as "good news from the other world". For a Dagara shaman such mental disorders are signs of two opposing energies merging in the same field. Disturbances are aggravated when those caught up in such a crisis are not given care and help when dealing with this conflict of energies.

Shaman Somé's experiment with the possible universality of the Dagara's belief that mental disorders are basically a spiritual phenomenon, focused on a young African-American by the name of Alex. Medicated and admitted to a psychiatric institution, Alex showed no signs of improvement, with debilitating depressive moods pressing heavily on his days and nights. With his parents' permission Shaman Somé brought the young Alex to Africa when he lived in the shaman's village on the border between Ghana and Burkina Faso. After about eight months in the village Alex's depressive symptoms lessened to where he showed no obvious signs of mental disorder. Alex spent four years in the village helping elders to interpret signs and helping with the healing of others. Translated through the wisdom of the Dagara, Alex was realigning his own personal energy with the energy force possessing him.

Through ritual, Alex shared the messages communicated to him by spirits and by what accounts we have he returned to America a healed man, satisfying Shaman Somé regarding the universality of the Dagara's healing system. Back in America Alex went on to study psychology in university even though those who knew him had doubts about his ability to even complete high school. Shaman Somé described Alex's experiences as coming from someone who:

> ... was reaching out. It was an emergency call. His job and his purpose was to be a healer. He said no one was paying attention to that.

A recurring theme in mental disorders is identified by Shaman Somé as an ancient ancestral trace. This trace of energy is uncared for and perverted so it makes itself known in the mortal personality. The outcomes are often very negative. Shaman Somé believes that the high rates of mental illness in the west are connected to the thwarted spiritual energy of nature, convoluted by machines and compounded by a disconnection from the spirits of the past. He says that it's not so much what the person wants, but rather what the spirit wants.

> The spirit sees in us a call for something grand, something that will make life meaningful and so the spirit is responding to that. There is a strong longing for a profound connection that transcends materialism and possessions of things and moves into a tangible cosmic dimension. Most of this longing is unconscious, but for spirits, conscious or unconscious doesn't make any difference. To say that ritual is needed in the Western world is an understatement. We have seen in our own people that it is probably impossible to live a sane life without it.

Although the complexities of Western nations are dissimilar to life in a rural African village, the questioning mind is gripped by the shaman's view that those in mental distress are called by spirits from the other worlds to cooperate with them in doing healing work.

Given time, training, and education, could the clinician working in the west possibly save lives by merging sacred and ritualised methodologies with mental disorder treatments, rather than negating so much of the sufferer's humanity by reducing it to the focus of pathological study and pharmaceutical experiment? In indigenous cultures throughout the world young people are initiated into adulthood when they reach a certain age, a suggestible age between boyhood and manhood, girlhood and womanhood. In so many post-industrial regions, the lack of such a ritual is part of a crisis of awareness. Shaman Somé reminds us that:

> Unless the relationship between the living and the dead is in balance chaos ensues. If these ancestors are not healed their sick energy will haunt the souls and psyches of those who are responsible for helping them.

Despondency is fixed in Kenny's eyes. What rites of initiation into adulthood has he known? Who prayed for him in the most abject hours of his suffering? What shaman advised him to remain at peace with the spirits of those gone before him? Who validated his voices by placing them outside pathology? What did the mushroom say to him at a time of crisis? I guess like so many others when the spiritual malaise first set in, he unwisely tried to kill it with the cure that is never more than an arm's length away, the wrong kind of synthetic drugs or alcohol, or some other variant of addiction. And in turn the mental and physical cost of toxicity became the polestar of therapeutic attention. Recreational drugs or synthetic drugs marketed by the pharmaceutical industry are only ever on the surface of a torrent of psychic energy.

Taken out of context, such chemicals and intoxicants cover up or make matters worse. Deep in our hearts we understand that the malaise is more many-sided than what research scientists tenured by pharmaceutical conglomerates can find remedies for. In the reception rooms of what mental health hospitals remain, there would never be time to ask the questions begging to be asked. Time itself becomes a commodity eaten up by monstrous appetites. The questions are endless, and, at the end of the questions, the heart of the matter is hardly touched.

Gestalt theory pioneer Fritz Perls baulked at the classic Freudian hypothesis of regression. In his early writings, a template for modern Gestalt practice, Perls reinterpreted the psychotherapeutic analysis which views adults who revert to unreasonable and childlike behaviour as regressing to earlier stages of comprehension. They are, Perls explained, showing their true selves:

> He does not regress to the state of his childhood anxiety. His nucleus, his true self, was never anything else but excitable, his underdevelopment has never ceased to exist.

Perls' reading of the Freudian notion of transference is likewise oppositional. For him the neurotic does not project foremost personalities from their own life onto the analyst or onto others in the therapeutic environment. Perls's idea has the neurotic projecting their own unconscious, ugly traits onto others. Say, for example, when the neurotic or patient in analysis is transferring a cruel, unloving father onto their clinical practitioner, they are projecting their own cruel, unloving traits:

> As a child he had projected his own intolerance onto the father … The whole complicated process, both aspects, the cruel father and the cruel analyst, boil down to the simple fact of projection of the unadmitted cruelty in the patient's own personality.

For the student of human anguish, such conclusions are of real worth. Perls's ideas nudge us away from the association of negative traits with our early socialisation. We move closer to the acceptance that repugnant or negative expressions and behaviour are more centred in the human character than anywhere else. The door is then opened to other ideas as to how the human character is distorted and misaligned with the principles and goals of civilisation, and how it can stall and mutate in its evolution. At this very moment of therapeutic exposure, the neurotic is faced with the psychic candour of their malaise. They are asked to digest the indigestible and in doing so accept the cause of moroseness as their own ugliness or underdevelopment of character.

In this revelation of clarity when the sovereignty of the human character is shining brighter, a wider span of probabilities comes into view. If the human character or personality does not reconcile itself to the classic psychosocial models introduced to the Western mind by the great innovators of psychology and psychiatry, then the gates to other worlds and to more varied happenings are opened.

One example used to support the idea of reincarnation is the great composer Mozart. By the age of three Mozart was already showing uncommon musical aptitude. By the age of eight his musical gifts were advanced to the standards of a gifted Master of Music with decades of musical accomplishment behind him. It was as if the spirit of a skilled musician had descended on the infant Mozart and then the Master of Music's Work continued through the precociousness of the child. Many cultures and spiritual traditions throughout the world accept this view as quite normal. It is often used to explain traits and characteristics at the hub of human personality. These traits and characteristics often go unexplained or passed over without comment in Western and Westernised lands or else are shrouded in psychobabble or overly simplified with reductive biology.

Conversely, if it is imaginable as part of the wisdom of humankind for the spiritual kernel of a departed person of exceptionable character to influence the living personality of another human being, then what about the spirit of an ugly and debased nature having a harmful effect on a living person? Research in this field is now more coherent and, depending on an individual's parameters of reference, more credible.

Personally these ideas did not begin in any given religious, spiritual, or personal belief in reincarnation, or in a fixed belief in one of the fields of study which tease human curiosity from the margins of science and metaphysics. They arrived in my mind through years of supporting distraught and often desperate people in the working boroughs of London, separate from any interest in holistic therapies and the arcane. They incubated after weighing up several ideas about what it is to be human.

It was often a large elephant in a rather cramped room. The verbal dynamics of our accepted psychology and social care models could only at best dance around the question of a personality from another plane of life as present as those of us who are here in physical form. The genius in Western thought can only be magnified by the fullest engagement with the world of ideas, be they centred here in the west, or elsewhere. In our own history so many esoteric gems and astounding ideas were muted, deleted, or redacted by the strangest fads and twists of fate and chance. I mention all this as I am on my way to see Peter. He lives on one of those inner-city housing estates which occasionally make it into the headlines when someone is stabbed or shot.

There is an abandoned red brick Anglican Church with its doors and windows locked and shuttered, and what could be called an industrial estate with rows of lockups with lopsided doors and rusted hinges. There is a basketball court and a five-a-side football pitch behind chicken-wire. Concrete laneways zigzag here and there. For all its reputation, everything is controlled, observed and regulated. Neighbourhood police, community support officers, wardens and the local authority's social inclusion teams know the ground well. Nobody gets away with not paying a bill or a traffic ticket, or not renewing their television licence. Nobody living here can skip a magistrate's court appearance or a bailiff's visit. This is not the 1990s so there are no squatters. The tentacles of the state are, it would seem, even more pressing here than anywhere else.

The perception of these housing estates as dangerous and as places where the outsider takes their life in their hands is mostly another media and societal construct. The people who live here must conform and pay their dues, just as you and I must conform and pay our dues. An abiding problem in such neighbourhoods is how so many people who live here spend inordinate levels of energy and time at work and travelling to and from work. Municipal workers, bus-drivers, care-workers, and NHS hospital cleaners live here. They are limited in the time they can spend with their growing children and in the hours they can share in family life. This sacrifice to the gods of employment is one of the causal factors of youth gang culture, since without a loving family to be part of and a meaningful role in that family, where can the young turn? Others fall to the social ills and maladies none of us are immune to. There's a sense of claustrophobia due to the lack of space and the absence of a connection to nature.

We are masters of our unsaid words and slaves to the words we have let slip unwisely. Peter understands this old truism as much as anyone does and he is canny in what he says. He has been recycled through the various stages of the psychiatric system and is still around to talk about it. The neurotoxic effects of alcohol have left him a little stunned and groggy, but for all this self-inflicted punishment his mind is remarkably intact. He welcomes me with a sneer at the door of his second-floor flat and sticks out a limp, damp, insanitary hand. It is a challenge to grip it without showing any outward signs of disgust.

The reason Perls came to mind on my way to see Peter is because when Perls wrote about the unadmitted cruelty in the patient's own personality, he was most likely thinking about someone like Peter. There is an unpleasantness to the man that he sometimes tries but never comes anywhere near containing. He is in his early fifties and looks older as he has neglected himself through the indifference familiar to people who have lost touch with everyday society, employment responsibilities, and intimate relationships. His flat is a cesspit of neglect. In earlier times he'd have been evicted and signed over to the care of an institution or long-stay hospital. He pushes the boundaries of every human relationship he's even remotely involved in but knows just where to draw the line. The council have threatened to evict him several times, and each time he said and did enough to satisfy them that he was going to change his ways and go along with their rules and recommendations. He uses his mental health history like a club to bash his way out so many of the situations that his rage, casual hatred of nearly everyone he comes into contact with, and his insults to others land him in.

He terrorises neighbours and breaks every rule in his tenancy agreement. Several times the police have dragged him out of his flat in handcuffs. Typically he had been drunk on cheap cider and after drying him out in the cells they would send him home with a caution. There is a young mother with an infant in the flat just below. She suffers from his failure to control real or imagined demons rampaging in his mind, and a random housing allocation which housed her so close to someone like him.

As this neighbour peeped from behind her front-door the fear in her eyes couldn't have been more real. She came across as a reasonable person and a very devoted mother, but fate had housed her in a council flat beneath someone like Peter. She did not have to explain it, as her dilemma was very understandable. She did not have the financial means or the family support to move somewhere else. And nobody in their right mind would ever swap with her through the council's home-swap scheme.

Nobody wants to live in a flat anywhere near someone like Peter. Yet since the policy of deinstitutionalisation became the salient virtue of social care and psychiatric aftercare, many tens of thousands of people have no choice but to live next to somebody like him. In conversations with experienced and gifted community mental health workers they parroted the wisdom from on high. It is a wisdom consigning ever more adults to solitary flats they cannot manage, in a community they are not part of. The care in question is desultory and the term "community" is mostly not a real thing. The common view is that economic imperative shapes every word spoken in any conversation by policymakers to do with mental health or social care policy. The high staff turnover in frontline staff can be analysed in statistics if anyone is still unconvinced that something is seriously wrong.

As part of the general wisdom of deinstitutionalisation, people with mental disorders who can't look after themselves are sent to live in ordinary flats in many cases with very little if any real support. A high percentage of the outpatients our mental health charity is contracted to care for cannot manage to live on their own. The house where Gareth lives near St. Thomas' Hospital is an exception, a humane place of minimal care and support. But often neighbours go through hell as more mentally disordered men and women are given the keys to flats and bedsits they have no hope of keeping in any kind of fit condition.

In one case neighbours literally begged me to help. They knew I'd been sent by social services to support the mental health outpatient in question and couldn't understand why he'd been resettled in a normal block of council flats, when he clearly needed more specialised housing and care. It was hard to connect with this guy on any kind of regular basis as he would either ignore his doorbell or just wouldn't be around. Neighbours complained about the smell from the his flat. They were not exaggerating; standing anywhere near his front-door was just like standing next to an open sewer. Only the very brave of heart dared to open the letter-flap to take a peek inside. It was not a smell you would associate with civilised living.

The housing association did not have the keys to the heavy mortise lock on the front door so we couldn't get inside the flat. The neighbours were insistent, demanding that the flat be checked to find out just what exactly was causing the smell. They had to cover their mouths and noses when they passed anywhere near it. The mental health coordinator who had joined me on the visit called the police and a young constable showed up and volunteered to climb in a back window just within reach from a low roof by the side of the building. The constable squeezed in the bathroom window but slipped as he tried to find a footing inside the bathroom, tumbling into a bathtub filled with faeces and urine. The toilet was blocked and overflowing with faeces and there was no sign of the mental health outpatient as he often slept rough in the centre of London for weeks at a time. The flat was indescribably filthy.

The constable opened the flat door from the inside to let me and the NHS care-coordinator in, then he went back to the station to clean the faeces and urine of a sick man from his uniform and body. Someone said the constable handed in his resignation as soon as he had cleaned himself up, but I don't know for sure if he did. If he had joined the Metropolitan Police to fight crime and keep the streets safe he would not have liked the job of picking up the pieces of disastrous political decisions which abandon so many mentally disordered people and dump mental health outpatients who can't care for themselves into sensitively located general needs housing.

Neighbours go through hell, just as Peter's neighbours go through hell. Politicians and senior commissioning managers who closed the asylums and mental institutions, support services, and daycentres, and who reduce the number of mental health beds each year, are responsible for so much of this. But they themselves and their immediate circle don't have to live in a council block next door to somebody like Peter. If they did, our mental health policies would change quickly. The curse of hierarchies and our human tendency towards self-centredness follows all of us through time.

The key points of ancient Gnostic and esoteric thought are sublime, and when the penny drops, they can shift to one side many of the simplifications that prop up a civilisation, so that the mind can focus on something more wondrous. It is not the easiest subject to mention in this context, because it is hard to look to anything outside the brutal truth of each task. It is naïve to think ancient thought can be in any way helpful to mental health outpatients like Peter, but some knowledge of arcane worldviews can help us to deal with the suffering of the world. Gnostic schools of the ancient world shared general principles such as the conclusion that we are confined to cycles of birth and death in a material world. We are fallen beings but inside all of us is the trace of our prototypical divinity. This spark of the divine remains inactive until a revelatory knowledge known as *gnosis* lifts each mortal spark of divinity free from the material world.

Men and women of the earth were once elevated spirits, aeons that tragically fell from the pleroma, the place of light, into a universe of material existence at odds with our actual essence and material reality. Every fallen spirit is imprisoned in a mortal body of flesh and bone, and to escape this fate the gnostic turns within, to the divine parts of us which are the marks of our original godliness. This division of body and soul is the kernel of a troubled dualism, a schism between the eternal soul and the material and often depraved world our bodies imprison us in.

Only spiritual knowledge known as gnosis—and not faith or convoluted doctrines administered by a politically-minded priesthood or by dissenting laity who run in tangents with bizarre ideas lifted from scripture—can liberate us from our human bondage and return us to the spiritual domain from whence we came. Gnosis is a deeply personal unfolding, where through meditation, reflective thought, and study, it comes to us as an Orphic realisation, a revelation of spirit and mind. It is mystical and ecstatic, an advent of great light after an impasse of darkness and confusion. It manifests in the mysticism of the world's great faiths.

Gnostic mythologies charted spiritual journeys from darkness to light. For the modernist interested in the spiritual refinements of ancient creeds so much of the psychic torment of our world can present as the conflict between the material world and the divine spark inside all of us. At times certain episodes of what we understand as mental illness can seem like an eruption of arcane tension, the antipathy between the spiritual element inside us and the often violent material world created by a demiurge. Speculating on whether or not an ignorant demiurge rather than an omnipotent God created people like Peter, people like all of us, is somehow reassuring.

Peter is ranting on about his rights, jutting an angry, unclean finger into the air. He plays the same old game all the time, and scores the same tired points, bad-mouthing a worker from one of the public sector agencies involved in his case. In the next breath he grudgingly admits another worker is not so bad and at least tries his best. He is forever manipulating the social worker who coordinates his care and likewise the community alcohol rehabilitation worker and social care workers who are unfortunate enough to have an input into his care. He asks if I would like a coffee and I say no thanks, but he says I should have one anyway and puts the kettle on. Reluctantly I sit on the edge of a dirty chair in the absence of anywhere else to sit.

He is angry and shouts about an alcohol worker I have never met, and insults her through bared, yellowing teeth. He is angrier as he goes on to talk about an imagined slight from the worker he despises. Nothing I say is getting through to him. All this foolishness is taking us away from the work that needs doing, the usual banal but necessary mental health support work that requires just a little cooperation and engagement. He is a disquieting man and his energy projections are far removed from anything close to peace or integration. He is lurching from one side to the next in front of me, a kettle of boiled water in one hand, ranting about an alcohol worker from a local authority day-programme. He wants the world to fit itself to his childish and angry demands rather than adapting to the world as he finds it.

Finding a filthy cup, he tips a measure of coffee straight from the jar into it and carelessly adds boiling water. He spills more on the floor than he manages to pour into the cup. Offering the filthy cup with the graciousness of a thug, he stands right in front of me, so I understand he is holding a kettle of boiling water not far from my head and face. Just a quick jerk of his arm would scald my face and head and perhaps maim me for life. Words of anger are escaping him. I take the cup from his hand and place it on the floor by the chair where I sit and change the subject. Placing the kettle where it usually stands, he lets out a yobbish, sneering laugh.

In polite circles we can sometimes hear the self-congratulatory assurances, in keeping with the progressive idea that at one time we burnt people as witches when they were really suffering from mental illnesses.

The supine implications of such generalisations are to link psychiatric innovation with brutish imprints in the popular mind of Elizabethans burning Lollards at the stake, or Hopkins the Witchfinder General skulking from village to village in East Anglia. Attitudes to mental disorder and what we now refer to as diversity could be as inhumane as much as they were unreasonable, abusive, and unscientific.

The natural progression of a conversation when this association is raised tilts towards a simplification of arcane methods of spiritual healing, both pagan and Christian, in the British Isles and in a wider European context. Standards of modern Western psychiatry may be referenced. This selective reading of cultural and medical history revitalises a mythology cobbled together in the twentieth century which promotes Western psychiatry to the peaks of human enlightenment and medical achievement.

We can take the cultural medicine in a single gulp like many do and allow a hierarchy of psychiatrists, psychologists, and commentators to do our thinking for us. Or we can look more closely at oral history, folklore, customs, and fables. A wider quest leads us to pagan, pre-pagan and cunning folk rites, cures, and arcane readings of demonic possession. In moving from folk, spiritual, cultural, and religious symbolism to the new gods of secularism and science, the care and treatment of mental disorders forgot its most insightful and persuasive precepts.

A culture so quick to forget so much of the wisdom of those who were once living is a culture more predisposed to meaningless fads, false thinking, unnecessary confusion, and wild notions which subject the human mind to simulacra of the new religion of scientific advancement and its technological wonders. The scale of suffering of our mentally disordered is rarely investigated as a factor of the disconnections between who we are now and those who went before us. Our cultural wisdom often only stands on the shoulders of our present generation, with the wisdom of generations past lost to a bewildering pace of change.

Have we moved too fast in separating ourselves from the spiritual significance of mountains and rivers, from holy wells, sacred trees, and ancestral lands that were then taken from the people and now form the basis of the wealth and privilege of a handful of titled families? What exactly did we lose on the journey from feudalism to industrialism, and from industrialism to post-industrialism, and to this present time with its prophets of nihilism and reductive codes of materialism? With the history of cruelty and violence against the human spirit in mind, none of this is surprising. The truth as we find it is that we do not know how to react to the casualties of a structure of living stripped of ritual. It can appear that we have bartered a wealth of cultural wisdom, love of Godhead, and pagan reverence for nature for a reductive cosmology that doesn't help us in any way, and a materialist way of looking at things that is incompatible with the sanity needed for the healthy continuation of future generations.

We may have already reached a point where we cannot allow ourselves to indulge in the idea of unsympathetic communications from a consciousness not centred in the human mind as a possible cause of mental disorder. To do so would be to offend the princes of the materialist philosophy informing so much of what is accepted as good practice. Psychiatric assessors in the NHS and its private-sector adjuncts dare not listen to the wisdom of the African shaman, the Jungian dreamkeeper, the family member who believes in miracles, or the panpsychic freethinker. Their role is not to empower individuals by telling them they are healers, who are bringing good news from other worlds, or to tell them they are mentally disordered because of an absence of ritual and because of so much disconnection with nature in our culture and because of the ignorance in how we relate to those who went before us. Nor it is their duty to ask the sufferer to mull over whether or not their apathy might be related to spiritual ill will linked to those who went before us, or to ruptures in kinship bonds.

Psychiatric workers are there to encourage those reporting sick on mental health grounds to get over their depression or their tendency to break down into tears nearly all the time, or to snap out of their delusions, so they can return to the workplace as soon as possible. They are there to encourage workers, carers, and parents to resume a normal societal role. They are also there to promote medication to generate profit for pharmaceutical conglomerates. They are also there to promote the policy of Care in the Community, or deinstitutionalisation, over all other approaches in the face of growing criticism of such policies. The Centre for Social Justice condemned Care in the Community as a £100 billion pound failure, and commentators from both left and right of the political spectrum are equally hostile.

As gifted, humane, educated, and insightful as many of our NHS mental health professionals are, they are constricted by a model of care, that submits to the economic imperative of hyper-consumerism, and the delusions of a technologically distracted age. If they had the time and encouragement to explore the fuller inferences of the genesis of mental disorder, they would do so commendably. If they were freed from reductive biological modelling and the spiritual and intellectual myopia of their profession, to explore parapsychology and links between delusional behaviour and a consciousness outside the human mind, then they would probably excel at doing so. If they were invited to explore alternative cultural and holistic perspectives on where the mentally disordered are situated, they would do so with positive results.

There is work outstanding with Peter, practical work which he really should take an interest in. I have been through his paperwork and discovered that his mother left him quite a lot of money, which is held in a trust managed by his brother. He also technically owns half of the large London semi-detached house in a leafy avenue where his brother lives. This wealth, although it is not readily to hand, has implications for the state benefits he gets. In the generic role of a voluntary sector mental health worker, I am obliged to sort out this bureaucratic mess, as there is a likelihood that he is not declaring the fuller truth of his financial affairs. As such he may be breaking the law. Today's masquerade involves the pretence that anyone of us out here in these fields of misery can convince Peter to be a nicer and more agreeable person. Of course we can't.

Out here in the refined suffering of an advanced society, certain psychological schools of thought can help. The Gestalt approach to human distress is existentialism in action, at least in its braver interpretations. Modern Gestalt practice can seem indistinguishable from related fields, as it merges mainstream therapeutic principles with the primary ideas of the movement's innovators. The generic process is often referred to as integrative counselling. But an emphasis on awareness remains central to Gestalt. Through redirecting Peter's angry and neurotic projections to the ideal of his own existence, there is always the hope that his awareness of his own truer self will mature. Theoretically an expanded awareness can help us understand how our projections are nearly always an unlovely aspect or other of our true personality. One of the pioneers of Gestalt therapy Fritz Perls sees it thus:

> In general it can be said that whenever you feel jealous, suspicious, unjustly treated, victimised or querulous you can lay heavy odds that you are projecting, perhaps even that you are a paranoid character.

To try to get anywhere near the kind of maturation of personality required, Peter needs a series of life experiences to change his consciousness. Life changes us, all of us. Are any of us immune to humiliations we remember long after they have passed? Life disciplines us, and our suffering modifies the spirit like healing balm on a wound. Regardless of this man's anger and negativity, there is always hope that a breakthrough in awareness will help him move on from where he is. Even down here at this grade of life, there is always the hope of an awakening. However overlooked it may be by the reasoning of the arcane, a divine spark from an unknowable god amounts to as much in him as it does in any of us.

I try to talk to him about his finances, but he's not interested. He refuses to go there, waves it away out of hand, and insists that his social worker is dealing with it, even though I have assured him his social worker has passed it onto me. He is offhand and obnoxiously so. It's pointless. He wants to do nothing or speak of nothing but his repugnant projections about the alcohol worker he has taken a dislike to. It is a waste of breath trying to raise the other pieces of work I am hoping to make headway with. He prowls the flat shouting out louder and yet louder as his projections escalate. It is time to go. It serves no purpose to stay any longer.

To work day in and day out with such disturbed outpatients, the frontline worker must be strong enough to put up with protracted resentment and projection. We must be strong enough to survive attacks aimed at anyone who dares to try and guide the damaged psyche towards improvement or conformity, or even towards rationality. And to be able to enter the battle on another day, sometimes we must withdraw. Peter is awkward as I am leaving. He refuses to sign the contact-sheet the mental health charity insists he must sign on every visit, so it goes unsigned. As I leave, he follows me out onto the landing of the block of flats and raises his voice, demanding I do what he wants me to do. It is his favourite tactic, to deflect the task of actually making any effort at all, much preferring to blame others and to project his cruelty and hatred onto them.

I take the stairs quickly and am soon out of view. On the ground-floor near the beginning of one of the housing estates' zigzagging alleyways I can hear echoes of his disturbing voice, his shouts loud and ugly on the ear. I think about his neighbours and how often they must listen to him shouting. I think about the young mother with the frail-looking infant who lives below him, and remember the look in her eyes, a terror real enough to conjure the creator of this world, the perpetually ignorant demiurge.

There is a voicemail on my phone, and other calls are coming in too. Mostly they are routine. Someone wants to know if I can drop a foodbank voucher off to them later in the day. A harassed social worker wants an update on someone who she has referred to our service, but who I have not yet had a chance to meet. Somebody else slashed a kitchen knife across her lower arm and wrist. And no, she says she is absolutely sure that she doesn't need to ring 999 and get herself to casualty in a hurry. She mentioned it before, that going across the arm with a blade is a cry for help but going down the arm towards the wrist is the real thing.

In exchanges during every working day I try to channel energy from meditation and arcane studies towards human need. It is as necessary as any other part of the job. When working with the mentally disordered on so many doorsteps of despair, it is important not to lose connections with our own sources of energy. I have seen colleagues simply falling apart due to stress, overwork, and frustration. They battled on, but the temple of energy in their own hearts dimmed. A dreaded morning came when they woke up to find they no longer had the will or the vitality to keep going in this line of work. It is not unusual for workers to go on even when they have lost the inspiration to. Workers with young children or other dependents and with rising rents or mortgages and the usual economic pressures to worry about often have no choice in the matter. Workers are tied to the wheel of work as Buddhists say we are tied to the wheel of suffering. They must march on through the psychic torture and rationalise it how they can.

I once worked on a team with a recently qualified approved social worker who signed up for extra shifts in a residential project. On her very first night a patient broke into the room of another patient and raped him. The screams were heard by the duty staff, but the door was double locked from the inside and they could not get in. They had to wait outside the room of rape listening to the screams and waiting for the police. When the police finally arrived, they broke the door down and the mental health rapist panicked and smashed a window. He tried to climb through, but only managed to almost disembowel himself on a thick shard of glass. It was a night of pain, blood and rape with screams spiralling into the urban darkness.

The rapist almost died of shock and loss of blood but recovered in time to stand trial. The newly qualified social worker never worked in mental health again. She said it wasn't worth it. The last I heard she had returned to the Windward Islands with her husband where they had invested in a seafood business. If the frontline worker does not protect themselves against negative energy, then without doubt they too will wake to a morning of dread, a morning when an entire world vanishes into a vortex of fear and stress. So with this immutable fact in mind, I take a little time to review the visit to Peter.

In *The Acts of the Apostles* we read about Saint Paul at Ephesus burning whatever books he could find concerning matters curious. The books in question were to do with casting spells and working out magical rituals. If this influential man went to such trouble to destroy arcane wisdom, then it must have been something worth hearing more about. The French master of the esoteric Éliphas Lévi was sombre around themes linked with Saint Paul's book burning:

> … wisdom and sanctity are needful for those who would direct the secret forces of nature without being broken thereby; that to play

> with such terrible weapons without understanding them was the act of a fool; and that swift and terrible death awaits those who profane the Sanctuary of Nature.

The human subject's existence and raiment is the basis of all spiritual exercises. The questions we ask, or don't ask, are the measure of the freedom we have, or would like to have. To live is to question and to question is to quest. Therefore every person is either a temple of learning or is denied the birthright of learning. Isn't very person allowed to look into the nature of life tempered by their own personal gifts, experiences, and perplexities? If we are not free spiritually, then what sense is there to the word "freedom"?

Restrictions and penalties against spiritual freedom in the name of conquest, literalist religion, or tyranny of one kind of other weave a lengthy narrative of suffering and oppression in history. The orientation of the healthy human spirit and psyche is intuitively focussed on growth, self-will, and improvement. Only generations of repression and the unavoidable reappearance in every generation of hierarchies compels humanity to genuflect to literalist orders of state-worship, brutish economics, and dogmatic manifestations of religion. The hardboiled literalist fanatic, with the same loathing for the spirit of freedom as the totalitarian, corrupts all the saner concepts of God. Yet a significant percentage of every population sacrifices so much personal freedom for the bread and circuses of whatever hierarchy has managed to take and then hold onto power.

The percentage of any given population at any given time that aspires towards gnosis learns that there are limits to spiritual freedom. The esoteric path is distrusted by literalists and good people who are uncomfortable with the idea of thinking through each tradition of faith. There are religious extremists too, or others who benefit from censorship. And there are plenty who laugh off everything transcendental, gnostic, or different to what is held up as acceptable. Esotericists are also ridiculed by worldly religionists who willingly misread the arcane as devil-worshipping or soothsaying of the worse kind. Even in this time of relative enlightenment and tolerance, the intentions of the student of the arcane are misunderstood or misrepresented in an eyeblink. In so many avenues of society it is best for the experimentalist to say nothing at all.

After visiting Peter I need to purge myself of the influence of demons and the fetid astral energy of the man's aura. I know for the sake of my own spiritual energy I should use the Banishing Ritual, and later use yet more familiar mantras for consolidation, or say the Lord's Prayer repeatedly. On the walk to the bus stop I concentrate on breathing in through my nose and out through my mouth. At the bus stop my phone rings but I allow the call to go to voicemail. I don't feel concerned about not answering a possibly urgent call. I only have to think about a legion of workers from the past who were demoralised and over time were simply broken through stress at work. When I think of them, I understand more that there are ways of surviving this line of work and that there are ways of not surviving it.

On the bus journey to the office the phone rings again, and again I ignore it. I close my eyes and visualise a pentagram of luminous blue light. Holding the thought, I concentrate on an inner light and the visualisation magnifies. After a minute or two it becomes part of my mind. I concentrate and hold the image of the pentagram in place. The blueness of its lines becomes mesmeric and I am less aware of the sounds in the crowded bus and of the presence of others. I concentrate as much mental power as possible and enlarge the pentagram as the bus jolts over a series of potholes that belong more to a city at war than to one meant to be at peace. I withdraw deeper into self. I am just another weary and dozing Londoner but inside I'm connecting with the pentagram, and the visions of the Rosy Cross and the God of all our hearts. Somewhere in a doze, between sleep and wakefulness, the blue lines of the pentagram are now more real than anything else in the kingdom of the senses.

The visualisation is surprisingly good. The pentagram merges with the inner-eye and is now part of reality. Thus it becomes possible to imagine what it is like to step through the blue luminous lines, like stepping through an open window. And more fields of the imagination are then within reach, and beyond them the Astral Plane. And further on, there are intriguing spheres of light. But the bus is jolting again and there is an ugly exchange of words between two passengers with their voices bristling with the irritations of the day. There is now a poisonous vibe in the bus, but there is only a minute or two to go until my stop.

Stepping from the bus and taking a shortcut through an alleyway saturated by the stale urine of beer-drinkers on their way home from last night's pubs, a new font of energy surges from my psyche. The brief visualisation has done wonders. The spirit inside is lighter, less profaned by Peter's demons and by his demon-disordered thoughts. His problems are grounded not only in his psychology but in a disharmony in his energy fields. It is a disharmony mostly to do with destructive interference from what students of the arcane understand as the Astral Plane.

Workers who deal with all this day in and day out absorb these energies into their very bones and take whatever suffering that goes with it on the chin, trying not to think about the inevitable day when they wake up to burnout. They will then be unable even to climb out of bed and will be lucky to continue in this line of work at all. To detoxify psychically is as important as physical rest, for more prevails in the world than can be seen with mortal eyes or weighed by the imperial standard.

Nicos

Something is happening with Tina. I meet with the coordinator of the alcohol team to ask her to take another look at her care plan. They are not happy with the number of detox hospitalisations she has had in the past. They are not sure she is motivated to stay sober for even a single day, if she is given another detox. It happens; people walk out of detox wards after the first day or even the first hour, which irks NHS ward staff. I make her case with more conviction, assuring the alcohol worker that I will personally take her to the alcohol groups and make sure she gets there on time. The groups are run twice-weekly in the annex of what was once a functioning hospital, but now is home to several community-based medical teams and research projects. She hems and haws but agrees that if Tina shows up twice a week at the alcohol groups, then she is back on the list for detox. I thank her, promise I will make every effort to get her ready for detox. The alcohol team-coordinator comes across as a compassionate person, but she carries an air of jaded frustration around with her. Is she secretly longing to be elsewhere, away from all this prolonged misery and angst? Where does she want to be?

I ring Tina and then I ring her partner. I explain to both of them that a door has opened and that the alcohol groups at the former hospital are a route into detox. She is pleased. Having listened closely to her voice on the other end of the line, I sense it might be the last real chance she will ever have. I update them both on the housing situation as it's important for the sake of their welfare and health to get out of the slum they are in. The council is immovable, refusing point-blank to help, but I have spoken with a private landlord and there is a reasonable chance he can offer Tina and her partner a one-bed rented flat. She is over the moon at this news. But when I mention the area the landlord usually rents his flats in, she goes quiet. She says she will need time to think it over. It's understandable. The area has a lousy name. Nobody wants to live there. They need time to talk themselves into it.

At least there's something constructive happening for her. If she can make it to the alcohol groups and reduce her drinking a little, and if they see her face-to-face a few times, she will be on the list for detox again. And she is at a stage in her alcoholism where every mouthful of booze, every word said in her presence, and everything happening around her has a bearing on her chances of survival. In her case the esotericist might invoke light from the stars and the moon for strength to re-direct energy from the very heavens into her consciousness. In a holistic sense her overall environment and her partner and friends are a hindrance to her moving forward. If this boozing lark goes on much longer her human days are numbered in double figures, and draped from morning to night in physical pain, organ failure, morbidity, and humiliation. So often we are simply helpless in the face of such addiction.

Only once did we talk about her deeper aspirations. It was one of those conversations which can spring right out of nowhere. It was during the morning when I had brought her to the council housing office. They had insisted on seeing her in person even though they knew how ill she had been. And they had done nothing for her anyway other than waste her time filling in a stack of questionnaires that had been filled in and submitted already.

As we waited in reception to see a housing officer, she asked me if I believed in God. I said yes, I believe in God. I said I believe in miracles and the truth in scriptures, as long as they are not part of any kind of weird, unbalanced or controlling literalist agenda. I said it's quite a personal thing. She didn't really understand what I meant. I didn't trouble her by mentioning a development in thought over some years from an unknowable god to gnosis and paganism and deism and Spinoza's god. She said she used to love going to church as a child when she stayed with her grandparents, but as an adult there was never the time. And anyhow she would feel awkward and phoney walking into a church as an adult since she had lost her childhood innocence long ago. Churches she said are places really meant for children, or for people almost as blameless as children.

I asked if she'd like me to take her to a church or to arrange for a vicar to visit her at home. She said I needn't go to any such trouble. She had been to churches as a child and remembered how it felt and didn't want to risk losing special memories by going there as an adult. And she hated the idea of people visiting her at home as she was ashamed of the squalor. But if I managed to find them somewhere else to live then she would rethink the idea of a visit from a minister. Her spirit belongs with the angels. She is worlds away from this plane with its armies of money-counters and so many demons in human shape. There is so much suffering in her eyes yet her spirit shines through. She needs a masquerade as well, because when it comes to certain addictions there is often not much that can be done.

Miracles happen. And they happen every day in manifold ways, but mostly we are looking in another direction when they happen. With the busy lives we lead, it is harder to see miracles, so if one happens right in front of our noses, we tend to shrug it off as just another coincidence. Or we won't notice at all. With Tina her only real hope is a miracle. It doesn't take an expert in addictions to see she is fast slipping away from this world.

Are the truths we are searching for so often wrongly linked with human expectations? A modern philosopher once positioned the word "expediency" as the opposite of "morality". The reader might expect to read "immorality" as the opposite of "morality", but societies and their values move on quickly. In his *Two Concepts of Liberty* essay, Isaiah Berlin is at odds with the search for moral clarity and universality. Berlin did not seem to rate Kant's outer and inner perceptions; transcendent man with his bestial nature. He was not a fan of Plato's *Forms* and their moral implications either. Berlin's essay is more in synch with the Freudian idea of integrating logic or rationale from wherever we can find it with the more primitive characteristics of human identity.

In a mutation of Western thought in the twentieth and twenty-first centuries, there is a parting of the ways with the idealism of Plato and Kant, a new synthesis touched on by Berlin, a stepping back from moral universality and universal coherence. So much angst and dithering on so many questions to do with the transcendent are now anchored to the starker thoughts of Nietzsche and Schopenhauer and their present-day followers, or to the brutality of thought encoded in so many places as a culture's highest virtue by scientism.

The true enemy of a revised system of assessment and care for the mentally disordered is not so much moral relativism with its roots in the European Enlightenment that is now everywhere in the NHS and our social welfare systems, nor is it in the Nietzschean prophecy of nihilism that has come to pass in so many areas of Western life. Only a rigid, literalist monotheism or political tyranny unchecked by actual reality and secularism would really object to the ideas of Bergson, Jung, Rupert Sheldrake, or Malidoma Patrice Somé. Secular, liberal evaluations can only find fault with new interpretations of the arcane, when they are mistaken for the codes and absolutes of literalist religion. Otherwise, they can be made sense of as language games or projections from the id, or a question pitched to Zarathustra on his way down from the mountain.

It may be for the better if moral fanaticism is replaced by rationality and imperfect moral symbols unconnected to a quest for truth. Who could say for sure? But for now the outpatients under the care of our mental health charity are full of moral and spiritual aspirations, influenced to one degree or other by literalist monotheism and its history, along with its secular expositions. Or they are swayed by the humanism which followed on in the wake of a classic period of exoteric Christianity and Christian charity. Not to fully hear out the implied truth behind these aspirations would be needlessly cruel and shortsighted.

On another day Tina said she'd like to make it home for a week or so in the summer, as her only sister still lives there with her young family. For the sake of conversation, I asked her where she meant by home. Havering, she said. Her slight speech impediment and her natural accent meant that she pronounced the word in an odd way. When Kabbalists spell Jehovah's name backwards, the word means Satan. And when she mentioned the part of Greater London she was born and brought up in, it sounded like she had spoken the same word. I sat up straighter, conscious of a sudden tingling at the base of my spine. She was totally unaware of it of course, but it was as if a Kabbalist had used her lips to utter their secret word for Satan. What did it mean, if it meant anything at all?

Maybe it was just my imagination rather than her sweet way of pronouncing certain words. More likely it was nothing at all. But the word morphed into a mental picture of her poor health and crippling alcoholism and stuck with me for the remainder of the day. What surprised me, although looking back now it should not have surprised me at all, was how little faith her GP and alcohol workers had in the possibility of a recovery to transform her life. It was as if she was already dead in their eyes. Statistically the signs were not great.

Yet the life inside Tina is as much a part of the cosmic force uniting us all, as the life sustaining any other human being. Although eaten up by Jellinek's final stage of alcoholism, compounded by a grinding version of first-world poverty, she is a tough woman reaching out to others who are reaching out to her. The spark of the divine linking her to an unknowable god is as present in her as it is in all of us. And though it is not mentioned in NHS training manuals or the social care guidelines for England and Wales, miracles do happen. Or to put it another way, events happen which our modern codes of looking at the world have not quite named or worked out yet.

When I am worn down by people with killing addictions, Big Tam from Kings Cross comes to mind. He was not the type of person most people would want to spend time with. I was part of the team of drug and mental health workers with the job of rehabilitating him. Strong, tall, and violent he terrorised rough sleepers in pre-regeneration Kings Cross, necking litres of cider and jacking heroin into whatever veins were up to yet another hit. With two cousins just as menacing, he mugged, stole, threatened, and beat up other men down in the lowest gutters of life. Often Tam and his cousins roughed it in squats, derelict buildings, or crack houses. They were horrible apparitions in the Kings Cross of the time.

He almost killed a man right in front of me, his thumbs practically disappearing into the flesh of the man's neck. They were dug into his throat and Tam was squeezing harder and harder. Nobody can survive that kind of pressure. I knew a little about the guy Tam was choking to death, another hapless soul and street junkie. He too was a violent man who had only just got out of prison for stabbing a drug-dealer a few times with a pocket-knife. His face turned blue and he flapped about like an ugly fish, gutted and gasping for air. Although a strong man, he came nowhere near breaking Tam's death-grip on his throat. I jumped between them and the three of us swung around in a grotesque dance. Gripping Tam's wrists, I felt the unusual strength there. Then I applied a little pressure and used Tam's own weight to unbalance him. I shouted into his face from only a few inches away:

> Do you want to kill him?

He let go and lurched to one side. I let go of his wrists and stood between him and the hapless guy he had almost choked to death. I hoped it was over and that Tam would not come at me with boots and fists flailing. But I was ready for this too, willing if necessary to trade my blood for his blood right there on that miserable Kings Cross street. Sometimes in life such a moment arrives without warning. But it was not me he was angry with. I think somewhere in his tortured mind the reality of what had almost happened hit home. I had just stopped him from killing another man and having to sit out the long, unavoidable sentence that follows such a killing. The gasping man ran behind a nearby parked car with his face returning to a more normal colour, gagging harder, and then bending right over to vomit up a thin spout of green bile. Tam ranted on and on and waved a fist in the air. Then we heard a police siren. It was almost over and nobody had died. As the police siren came closer Tam calmed down a little and, ignoring me, he swung around and walked away without another word.

It wasn't an unusual incident in the Kings Cross of the time. Most shifts back then were about breaking up fights between pitiful needle users, and warning petty dealers and their runners to stay away from the front of the building. We faced down rage every day, breathed life back into those overdosed on heroin, and bandaged the cuts of self-harmers. They had lost so much control of their conscious will that they were functioning on raw emotion or instinct rather than anything related to rational thinking. They had given up on all the usual aspirations years before. The violence, rage and acting out never moved their lives forward in any way, at least not when you take the longer view. The violence, rage, and screaming aggression were mostly watersheds in a descent into the categories of hell people go through, on the very bottom rungs of life. The guy who had almost been choked to death did not mention Tam's name to the police when they showed up. He just said it was all a mistake and that he had been feeling unwell, shrugging it all off as a misunderstanding.

This incident faded quickly from the lively hours of those unlovely circles. There was always something more violent or degrading going on. A few weeks afterwards I bumped into Tam on Pentonville Road. We had almost walked into each other, so there wasn't any way of body-swerving him without him noticing it. He was oddly reflective and clean-shaven. He didn't smell of alcohol or look any more out of place than anyone else in the street. He wanted to talk. I was on my way to begin an afternoon-to-evening shift, so I didn't have a lot of time to talk. But I sat with him on a low wall bordering a housing block. He didn't actually apologise as apologies weren't any part of his vocabulary and he didn't thank me either for stopping him from killing that man.

He just rambled on in his Glaswegian drone about the boundaries of the world we both knew, when he was a subject of rehabilitation and I was one of those who were meant to be involved in some way in this rehabilitation. He spoke about another Kings Cross character who had just died from AIDS as he had ignored his diagnosis right up to his dying breath. He just blocked it from his mind and went on jacking up heroin to the very end. We spoke of others who had died from overdoses and others saved from the heroin needle by a prison term. He spoke in slow tones about what was happening around him. Without alcohol and with just enough drugs to hold him he could be articulate.

He didn't mention almost choking that guy to death and I sensed from him that he didn't want me to mention it either. In the middle of his reflections on the lives of the people we both knew, he surprised me by mentioning a book about ancient pagan sites. He had found it lying about on the shelves of a communal space in a homeless hostel. He had read almost half of it and was looking forward to reading the rest. It was the first time he had read anything at all since his release from prison two years before. His voice changed as he spoke about what he had read. It was clear that he was fascinated by the images in the book and the tales of serpent-gods and sacred trees. I said that I only knew a little about such things and, although I had read a bit about paganism I had forgotten much of it. I also found it absorbing. He quizzed me about what I knew and asked me more questions than I could answer. I had never seen him so intellectually animated before.

The incident where he almost choked a man to death had broken down the walls of uncertainty which can easily crop up between people in our roles. So, it did not seem intrusive when he asked me if I had ever used pagan rituals. Without analysing why he had asked me such a question I said I tried to view the world as open-mindedly as possible. He surprised me with more questions. This was Big Tam, the terror of Kings Cross, sounding like a little boy just about to open his Christmas presents. Both his cousins had left London in a hurry and were on the run in Scotland. The woman he had been hanging out with was locked up on remand and he stood before the world a more thoughtful man. A limited sense of awareness and a lack of self-control dimmed his cosmic light, but there must always be hope of growth in the human personality.

We spoke of pagans and animists and he listened carefully to every word I said. This was a side of him I had never seen before. I mentioned trips to Glastonbury, walks as far as the Tor, and conversations with people from the Pagan Federation. I mentioned a cunning man who used both pagan and Christian invocations, and who delved into the sacred rites of the ancients to shape his cures and simples. I pulled up one of the invocations on my phone and read it aloud. Again he listened to every word:

> I invoke you Headless One who created earth and heaven, who created night and day, who created light and darkness. You are Osoronnophis whom no one has ever seen. You are Iabas. You are Iapos. You distinguished the just and the unjust. You made female and male. You revealed seed and fruits. You caused people to love each other and to hate each other. I am the Headless daimon with my sight in my feet, the mighty one with the immortal fire; I am the truth that hates the fact that unjust deeds are done in the world, I am the one who makes the lightening flash and the thunder roll; I am the one whose sweat falls as rain so that it can inseminate the earth; I am the one whose mouth burns completely; I am the one who begets and destroys; I am the favour of the Aeon! My name is a heart encircled by a serpent. Come forth and follow.

There we were, me and Tam and millions more like us, searching in our own way for truth or meaning, or some kind of connection with what went before us. Or hoping a ritual will take us closer to where an inner voice is always quietly asking us to go. Taking whatever comfort in esoteric wisdom there is to take, we stumble and search at these urban crossroads. In a more sweeping notion of time, it is not so long ago when he might have found in the gems of his own native culture a cosmic vision of some vivacity. For those moments at least there wasn't any need to masquerade as someone else.

In the North of Scotland a few hundred years ago people prayed to a secret but nameless power. They knew about rituals to cure epilepsy and depression. In a landscape of sacred isles, holy standing stones, and healing wells, and with a syncretised pagan and Christian devotion, the Northern Scots imbibed culture and language in the same breath that they imbibed spirituality. In John Greenleaf Whittier's poem we hear the reiteration of a succour once known to Big Tam's forefathers:

> O restless heart and fevered brain,
> Unquiet and unstable,
> That holy well of Loch Maree
> Is more than idle fable.

Not all people honoured arcane codes in the British Isles of the past, especially many of those in authority. The Survey of Scottish Witchcraft records that on Orkney alone between 1594 and 1645 nineteen women and one man were charged with witchcraft. Nine of the nineteen were convicted and executed by strangling or burning. Elspeth Reoch was burnt alive after she confessed to dealing with fairies. Bessie Skebister was convicted of offences including shaking her hair loose at a woman who later became ill. According to one of the keepers of the Survey some of these accusations were very strange and could be as trivial as looking at someone in the wrong way. A paranoid fear of secret knowledge was in the air, a dread of esoteric wisdom hidden outside the citadels of authority and religious power. For the ignorance of an ignorant creator to thrive, the illuminations of wisdom must be doused, even if some of the innocent have to die or be tortured along the way. Native knowledge of the divine was eradicated by ignorance and fear of the unknowable before Tam's generation got to hear about it.

Big Tam, like many other citizens of the modern world, is a stranger to the wisdom of forefathers and the arcane consolation of tribal fealty. And as such he is more easily delivered to the confusion of the crossroads and its nihilistic or happy-pill philosophies. Like many millions more, he offers his soul on the tabernacle revered by the gods of globalised money and is eaten alive by the illusions of one too many crazed money-counters. Thus delivered, the secular gods blinded in their souls by an eternally ignorant creator can suck the marrow from his bones and obscure even more the divine spark within, put there by an unknowable god.

In a world so thoroughly mapped out by technology, much that was wondrous has been lost. Holy wells and wisdom of elders, sacred isles and invocations to a secret and nameless power are now missing from cultural perceptions. They were displaced by endless hours of televised outpourings of what can only be called immature egoism, comedians laughing at their own jokes and reality shows, and by interactive gadgets and the secular healing gods of pseudo-science and pharmacology. We create yet more technology, and fool ourselves into believing we control it, whereas it mostly controls us. Big Tam always knew a primal element was missing, and when he stumbled on a book about paganism, the embers of something ancient in his soul flamed into life. A chimera of the secret of the nameless one crossed before his inner eye.

I mention Big Tam because he was regarded by the many agencies who knew him as a hopeless case, and his presence in the world then was threatening and as close to hopeless as it gets. A few weeks after we had spoken about paganism and spirituality, he disappeared as if he had fallen into a deep crack in the earth's surface. One day he was terrorising the street-junkies and heroin-dealers of Kings Cross, and the next day he was gone. Only some time later through the charity mental health grapevine did we hear that he had finished a detox in a West of England town, followed by a long spell in residential rehab.

A few years later there was more news. Tam had stayed clean and abstinent and was working full-time in a hostel for ex-drug users. If anything, he proves there are no hopeless cases. Whenever I am reminded of him, I hope that he managed to find a way back to his own soul, to the beginning of the inner journey towards gnosis. And at times when working with Tina or Kenny or others at the very brink of life, Big Tam comes to mind as does his pagan-inspired awakening and transformation.

I am on my way to see Nicos. He's a faultlessly kind, troubled, gentle, highly-strung, and almost saintly man, who is close to retirement age, although he hasn't actually worked in his life. He pinpoints the day of disaster, which was at the beginning of the final year of a college accountancy course, when he had what he describes as a nervous breakdown. He has spent the decades since in and out of psychiatric wards. Several years ago, they handed him the keys of a small council flat in keeping with the principles of deinstitutionalisation.

Nicos is very religious and believes in miracles far more than he believes in the mental health system's abilities to heal him. Yet it doesn't stop him from fretting about every last detail of the care plan in place and asking question after detailed question about all matters even vaguely relating to him. He meets me at the door of his flat in worn tartan carpet-slippers, creased slacks, woollen cardigan with food-stains down the front of it, and a musty old shirt with a frayed collar. Wisps of white hair dangle on either side of his bald dome, and greyish-white stubble speaks of at least two mornings without a shave. Carrying a small wooden icon from the Greek Orthodox tradition, he passes it anxiously from one hand to the other.

He is waiting for the miracle to come, for his nervous health to be restored to some kind of normality. Through the decades he has had a small army of relatives and members of the Greek Orthodox community of North London praying for him, both in unison and in the privacy of their hearts. Noble and enlightened monks and magnificently bearded patriarchs in monasteries high in the mountains of Greece and among the hills of Cyprus have prayed for him. Pleas were made, sacrifices given, and novenas to Mary and the saints offered for the sake of Nicos's health. But to date the miracle has not happened.

William Godwin in his *Lives of the Necromancers* writes of a duality of belief:

> Nothing can be more memorable than the way in which belief and unbelief hold a divided empire over the human mind, our passions hurrying us into belief, at the same time that our intervals of sobriety suggest to us that it is all pure imposition.

In the real world Saul becomes Saint Paul every day. People wake in the middle of the night to cry *Eureka!* And on the following morning reconfigure their entire lives on the back of the revelation. Today's atheist is tomorrow's saint or mystic, and vice versa. And, as Godwin explains in that one sentence, our perceptions and beliefs change in harmony with how we feel on any given day, and in synch with the circumstances of our lives.

In a world of paradox and uncertainty, Nicos waits stoically for the miracle to transform his life. I sit in the living-room on a hard chair, and he sits on the only other chair on the far side of the room. I update him on the routine social care work I have been busy with on his behalf.

It is difficult to regard him as mentally ill as such, as his problems are centred not so much in his brain but in his entire body. It is not solely a question of dysfunction of the intellect, but of an overall fragility of mind and body.

It is as if his very lifeforce was diluted a long time ago and hopes of it ever finding its primary vigour and resilience fade with the days. He sits in front of me with his soft, long-suffering features lengthening, as the sorrow and melancholy so often a part of how he sees the world settle into a more fixed arrangement. We both know what is coming next. Nicos needs to talk about his depression and his ongoing thoughts of suicide. There is no skipping this dismal listening experience. It is one of the central chores of the job.

In a different scenario, who knows what results might be possible? With black hellebore and Saint John's wort and lots of sea-air and sun and in a sanctuary of ancient, mystical Christianity where monks who relate to others with practised patience are always on hand to listen, we might find a different man. But this is a departure from the demiurge's world. It is naïve to believe any of this is simply about what is good for Nicos.

He is tied to his difficulties like a goat tethered to a stake. There's only so much ground he can cover in any direction before the rope binding him is stretched to its limits. He has a psychiatrist and a GP and a care-manager from Social Services who would never in a million years hint at any other option for Nicos. They approve of his helplessness and from time to time alter his meds a little. They loosen or tighten the conditions of his care-plan or call yet another meeting with his welfare as the main point on the programme.

It all goes around in a circle with his helplessness and suffering the central feature in all exchanges. His elderly mother, younger brother, niece, and nephew actually work against him by repeating how important it is for him to always obey the doctors and social workers, and to always do what they tell him to do. His misery is fixed like a binding law of nature in the lives of all who know him. His only wish is to be as close to the Greek Orthodox Church as he humanly can be. His thoughts are fixed on a miracle cure and the vision of heaven, his eyes and voice impressions of tenderness when he speaks of his faith. It is not outside the gift of the world to arrange for him to live in a monastery in Greece or Cyprus. We know it happens. We know in other lands there are sanctuaries in church grounds and monasteries. I have known seekers from the Horn of Africa, who abandoned the burdens and illusions of London to rent a room in the hostels attached to the Orthodox churches of their homeland. There they found what they could not find here, the spiritual and psychic consolations unifying them with a greater cause.

People tired of the carnal world have asked for sanctuary in the shadows of the great religions for thousands of years. Such choices are absent in public sector work with troubled people here in this part of Europe. The upper echelons of management of the London mental health charities struggle, as much as the NHS and other government bodies struggle, with the tensions of a society where individuals are allowed freedom of divine and discarnate expression. Certain managers are set against the idea of any support or platform for religious or spiritual sentiment, or excursus of any kind. As a disposable worker masquerading as a box-ticker willing to listen, there is always the risk of being seen to be acting against the patient's care-plan by taking too much interest in their theistic or anagogic feelings. But I think it is worth risking anyway. As somebody from just outside what might be called mainstream religious tradition, it does not interest me personally. Doubting the accepted interpretations of the monotheistic religions does not mean we have to withdraw from the world of spirit and deeper psyche. The apostate must look closer at the words of the literalist, for in the lexicon of the true experimentalist all interpretation is a therapeutic mistake.

I came across an olive-wood cross in a street market with a leaflet fixed to it stating that the cross is carved from olive trees planted in the Holy Land. I bought it and, together with a small plastic jar of water from the River Jordan blessed by a patriarch of the Eastern Church, gave it to Nicos as a gift. He was very pleased and tells me he sleeps with the cross under his pillow and sprinkles his sleeping area each night with a few drops of the Jordan water. It is what makes him happiest, talking about the transcendent, and anything to do with the Church he loves so passionately.

I would be a total fraud to try and ignore the one part of Nicos's life he finds solace in. I would be selling my soul for the sake of a warped rule of neutrality cobbled from the cadres of politically correct policy-makers, so often petrified of finding themselves on the wrong side of the blame culture. Occasionally frontline workers find themselves at the same meetings as politically correct managers, as they do all they can to create public services and perceptions of public services in the likeness of their own fears, projections, and prejudices. They masquerade as anything other than what animates them, the most gruesome projections from the darker parts of their own psyches.

There is a moment in existential therapy where the patient or neurotic is guided from the miasma of false blame and bogus analysis to stare into the reality of their failure to initiate action in the world. Processing the angst that comes from excitement, the next logical step is using energy and personal will towards the goal of fulfilment of instincts, thoughts, values, and needs. Here the patient or neurotic arrives at the doors of self-realisation and awareness of what is possible, concentrating on self-interested action in the world. It is a moment of subjectivity which inches closer to the starting point of the Eastern concept of *satori*, or wakefulness of the spirit.

When the seeker after gnosis gets to the point where their will is taken away from the pettiness, boredom, and weariness of a typical day, the outcomes are nearly always interesting. With the power of the human will and with subconscious energies redirected towards a chosen goal, such outcomes can overstep expectations. What powers of concentration are possible can be devoted to redirecting the healing vitality of the cosmic into the blood and bones of the outpatients on the books of our mental health charity.

Visualising healers like Apollonius of Tyrana, Doctor Bach, Eugene del Mar, or Saint Cyprian of Carthage, it is then possible to use the human will to create a loop of psychic healing. The healer calls out the name *Shaddai El Hai*, a holy name related to illness in the physical body. *El Hai* can be used in healing someone at a distance from the world because of *Klippah Nogah*, a hardening of the heart through sickness or injury. In healing through the Names of God we are asked to meditate beforehand on the physical shape of the prime Hebrew letters, to look for an understanding of their meaning and power through visualising them. Gnostic healers also use the name *Yahweh Elohim Tzavaot* to inverse the karmic sources of illness and to invite the luminous council of *tzaddikim* and *maggidim* into the healing vibration. The eternal void in all directions is visualised, and the experienced healer can bring holy and luminous entities into the healing space.

As I sit with him, I use visualisation as he softly talks about the routines of his week, never far from losing control of his emotions. Anxious about almost everything and about everyone who even abstractly brushes up against his journey through life, he frets about the other mental health patients at a day centre he sometimes shows up at. Obsessing about a mental health nursing assistant who helps him with his meds, he sits so far forward on his chair that another millimetre or two will topple him face-first onto the floor.

He is close to tears. He is talking about the moment when his life was ruined. It is a recurring theme in his personal narrative, how he was young and strong and on the threshold of a career in accountancy when he was cut down, not by physical disease, but what he refers to as a nervous breakdown. He has never got over it, never moved on from the trauma, even though it is almost forty years since it happened. He rolls his head mournfully from side to side and closes his eyes, his face a subdued facade of sorrow. Hands closing tighter around the religious icon he carries with him, he begins to sob quietly.

There is no verbal therapy under the sun persuasive enough to make sense of the sobbing of this tender man. I have seen it before, weeping for the life he never had, for the wife and children he never knew, for the status in the London-Greek community he never won. As charity mental health workers, we are at a de facto distance from the NHS and their reverence for the gods of science and secularism, so are not necessarily obliged to take the role of science-worshipper or someone so paranoid about offending others that they become a parody of a person, with no core to their being. It is not really expected of me to offer a platitude or two picked from psychiatry's latest fad and passed gratefully down the food chain.

Our managers and senior managers defer to the NHS and its psychological models of practice with blind devotion, if they have time to defer to anything at all. They expect us workers on the ground to do the same. But largely due to infighting, disorganisation, overstretched resources, and the fact we are out on our own engaging with the mentally disordered and the addicted for the greater part of our working week, it is not realistic for managers to micro-manage us from day to day.

There is no monastery with a pious, white-bearded patriarch waiting with one hand raised in blessing to welcome him. Our options for losing ourselves in nature are limited by trespassing laws and private ownership along with the harsh weather of these islands. The last time I walked through the park close to where Nicos lives, a dog-walker let two fighting crossbreeds off the leash and the dogs ran in circles around me. I am used to dogs so there wasn't any problem. Luckily Nicos was not with me as it could have really upset him and pushed him over the edge. I stand and walk the short distance between us and take his hands in my hands. I close my eyes and concentrate and visualise the healing energy from the Astral Light filtering through my physical body and into his frail hands. It is a risk to cross the cultural and social care boundaries between us with physical contact, because for all his gentleness he is still a heavily medicated mental health outpatient. But his eyes are softer and he looks up at me with the same innocence he must have looked up to his father with years ago as a boy. I say the opening words of the prayer and on the third word he joins me:

> Our Father, who art in heaven …

We pray together and I release his moist, soft hands and place one hand on his shoulder. For a reason I don't understand, a fragment of Enochian magic shapes in my words:

> Move, therefore and shew yourselves! Open the mysteries of your creation. Be friendly unto me for I am a servant of the same God, the true worshipper of the highest.

He closes his eyes and lowers his head and, in the Greek of his Fathers, prays in a fervent mumble of devotion. I call out the beginning of one of the handful of prayers I can remember verbatim:

> Be favourable to me o ye powers of the Kingdom Divine. May glory and eternity be in my left and right hands so that I may attain to Victory.

We plead to the higher forces together in his flat with my hand on his shoulder and with his words tumbling out in rapid whispers. I end with the opening line of a prayer fixed in my mind from a time in the past:

> O *Chaith ha Kodosh*, cry aloud as an eagle, speak as a man, roar and bellow.

He looks up at me childishly and holds his icon tight to his chest and his eyes are yet softer. He smiles and thanks me, thanks me for praying with him as nobody else is keen to pray with him, even though words of divine praise are more prized by him than any other use of his time. I do not bother mentioning an interest in the arcane or in the power of arcane healing, as none of it matters in the context of spiritual intimacy. This is holism, a sharing of ideas rather than a handing down from above a set of ideas borrowed from the thoughts of others.

I have paperwork which requires his signature. Routine forms and questionnaires are just another small part of the universe of bureaucracy, which all of us in the public sector must forever flounder in. There is no need to mention the demiurge or the earthly obstructions to useful communication with the celestial planes. It's not necessary to mention any other difference in how we see things, or what a holistic approach really means. He signs the paperwork quickly for the short interlude of prayer has excited him. He asks if I would take him to the Greek Orthodox cathedral in Bayswater one day soon. I promise I will. He then asks if I think his prayers are heard and if God might show him mercy by returning his health and sanity. Before I have time to answer he asks if I would pray for him at some point in the week, and I assure him that I will.

For the modernist looking on, all this is probably inching too close to the exoteric religions so distrusted by progressive societies. If we accept that people crave religion because they need a place in the world where the self is not alienated, consumerised, or despised, then Nicos's yearnings are more understandable. The Messiah, the Man-God, has personally promised to save the wretched, the put-upon, the weak, and the outcasts. Why would the Messiah lie?

There is little hope for Nicos as the world stands. He is so fragile he knows he could not stand up alone against any of the challenges outside his own front door. There is no utopia, post-Marxian or otherwise, to protect his fragile self from the kind of individualism that's around today; the market forces and reductive conclusions born from a work ethic that has been distorted through the years by so many marketing sharks, and their art of making something worthless appear indispensable. Utopian ideas have not come to pass, at least not here in these urban spaces. Individuals are defined by their social roles, by their income and ability to show up in the morning to do certain jobs. To all appearances, fate and luck rule the world. If he is viewed by society's standards, then he measures up to little, if anything at all. He would be classified as a deficit, a drain on the state's resources. No masquerade on earth could save him. Naturally his only hope is to be seen in another setting, an endlessly forgiving and understanding context. For almost his entire life the Messiah's love and mercy have been his only hope.

As I am leaving, he thanks me again for the olive-wood cross and the blessed Jordan water I'd given him. He thanks me for taking the time to pray with him. After he closes the door and withdraws into his stuffy flat he will not see anyone for the rest of the day, and probably not on the following day. Somebody might ring in the evening, his mother most likely. Or his brother might send a text message, or his brother's son or daughter might send a text message or ring.

It dawns on me now that here before me is a mendicant without the assent and love of the faithful, a pilgrim without a shrine in sight, a living link with the higher callings of devotion to the supernal. In regions of India he would have found peace by the banks of the Ganges, or at Kerala. In the African heartlands he would have sat with the village shaman, throwing shells and bones in the shadows and talking about good news from the other world. Here in a restless European city of commerce, what he cherishes most must always be signed off as spiritual and cultural interests on a bored, mentally fatigued social worker's tick-list. To apply the six-inch ruler and the kitchen scales method of trying to appraise his life and aspirations is an act of psychological vandalism.

To separate spirituality from mental disorder, while insisting on reductive, analytical terms and pharmaceutical responses in which the mentally disordered are categorised, is perplexing to the ordinary mind not in thrall to the systems in place. We are meant to learn from Nicos, and so many other vulnerable souls sent to live among us. We are meant to learn about ourselves and about the weaknesses in our character. We are in such a hurry at this crossroads that it is harder to see the signs. Nicos is Jesus incarnate, his contest of flesh against spirit our contest of flesh against spirit.

Desmond

Jupiter is in its last tango with Libra. Pluto, Neptune, and Uranus are in a backwards spiral which can lead us to believe we are in a cycle of repetition: Nietzsche's eternal recurrence? There will be a full moon next week in Pisces, an omen of yet more uneasiness to come. The relationship between Jupiter and Scorpio a little later in the month is a brighter sign for the inner harmony so many of us are looking for. On the way to see Kenny with my thoughts still on the movements of the planets, my phone rings. It's a twenty-six-year-old guy who lives with bipolar disorder and has episodes of psychotic breakdown. He is phoning from a psychiatric hospital, as he's been taken there by the police and held under Section 2 of the Mental Health Act. His words are only just understandable because of the higher dose of meds they have given him. He went to the mental hospital where he had been sectioned several times in the past, and said he really wasn't feeling well. They sent him back home and told him to rest.

On the way home he went into a high-street supermarket and quickly took off all his clothes and began tearing the shelves apart, chucking whatever came to hand at whoever happened to be shopping in the nearby aisles. The police were called and they took him back to the same hospital where he had just been refused help, and this time he was admitted. The ceiling for admittance to a mental health ward is now far higher than the tortured cries of help from a mental health outpatient in crisis.

The guy asks me a question I can't really answer. He wants to know why he has mental health relapses when he is on medication. The meds reduce his quality of life, and he hardly has enough energy for the simple chores most men two or even three times his age could do without much trouble. When he is not on medication, he has bags of energy but has mental health relapses too, much like he has when he is on meds. I can't answer because I know what he wants me to say. I can't encourage him to stop taking meds because we are both in our own ways too compromised by the system. If I encouraged him to stop taking his medication, my managers would get to hear about it sooner or later.

He is too enmeshed in the system to find the kind of self-sufficiency he is speaking about, because his home and living depend on what the state gives him. He has never really worked in his life and went straight into the mental health system aged twenty from his second year at university. To find the kind of freedom from medication he is talking about, he would have to go off-grid, and he doesn't have the skills, contacts, resilience, or characteristics to do that. Sooner or later, he would be back on the secure ward. A life without medication is not likely, as things stand.

I listen to his numbed words and then change the subject. I tell him that when he gets out I will take him to this year's most talked about exhibition at Tate Britain. He has a passion for art almost on a par with Gareth from the house close to St. Thomas' Hospital. We could spend hours gazing at the Sickerts, Freuds, Bacons, and Auerbachs. He agrees and brightens up a little, asks if I can drop off shampoo and a few other bits and pieces to his hospital ward. At this crossroads our mental health work is reductive and practical. If the Archangel Gabriel is anywhere nearby, he might have sympathy for us, but his wings are clipped by the many beasts of necessity.

Kenny is sitting serenely in the most comfortable chair in his flat, smoking a roll-up cigarette. There is a twitch in one of his legs and he inhales so deeply that his cheekbones protrude at the climax of inhalation to give him the look of a living skeleton. He is unusually relaxed, waiting for the ritual to begin. He is serious about it too. On the table before me there is a collection of personal items. Kenny is convinced that these items connect him to the most damaging aspects of what happened earlier in his life. I have asked him to search through his belongings for links with the dread and failure of the past.

There is a psychiatrist's report, several letters from a mental hospital, and a passport-sized photo where Kenny's eyes are fixed in a medicalised stare familiar to mental health patients. There are several other old Kodak photos of various people who could be family members, the photos curled at the edges. There is the business card of a solicitor with a North London address, and letters too from the Department of Work and Pensions. There is a stack of folded-up letters from the Citizens Advice Bureau and a crumbled two-page mental health charity newsletter. There are at least a dozen letters in their original envelopes with stamps and postmarks dating back over a decade. The handwriting on the letters is remarkably neat and ornate like a calligrapher's font.

I take a roman candle, a box of matches, and a stick of sage incense from my rucksack, and place them on the table close to the stack of papers and photos. From a pocket I take a page of text and unfold it. All the while Kenny is watching me from the corner of one eye, one leg twitching. The rolled-up cigarette is never far from his lips. I strike the match and light the candle and then light the incense stick. In the following minutes I whirl the incense, imbuing the stuffy interior of Kenny's squalid flat with the influence of sage.

Ecosystems in the Mediterranean and the African savannah have mutated because of fire. Animals and plants evolve in response to fire. Certain seeds only germinate after they have been touched by fire. In Australia a raptor bird was observed picking up a burning stick from a bush fire. The raptor then carried the burning stick to some ground untouched by fire, dropping it close to a burrow in the hope of burning its prey out into the open.

I spread the page of text flat on the table and smooth it out. It is the *Hymn to the Sun* by the Neo-Platonist Proclus, published by Thomas Taylor in 1793. I take each piece of what represents Kenny's most negative impressions of the past and set it alight by touching it to the candle's flame. I then drop the fragment flaming into the nearby kitchen sink and wave the incense in the air with more vigour, sometimes tracing the shape of the pentagram, as I pronounce Proclus's words:

> Hear golden Titan! King of mental fire
> Ruler of light; to thee supreme belongs
> The splendid key of life's prolific fount;
> And from on high thy pour'st harmonic streams

In rich abundance into matter's worlds.
Hear! For high raised above the Astral Planes
And in the world's bright middle orb thou reign'st
While all things by thy sov'reign are filled
With mind-exciting, providential care.

I work methodically, careful not to burn my fingers on the papers and photos lit from the flame of the candle, then drop them burning into the aluminium sink. Kenny watches me all the while, expressionless and without comment.

The starry fires surround vig'rous fire.
And ever in unwearied, ceaseless dance
O'er earth wide-bosomed, vivid dew diffuse
Thy by perpetual and repeated course
The hours and seasons in succession rise;
And hostile elements their conflicts cease,
Soon as they view thy awful beams, great King;
From deity ineffable and secret born.
O best of gods, blest daemon crowned with fire
Image of Nature's all-producing good,
And the soul's leader to the realm of light,
Hear! And refine me from the stains of guilt.
The supplication of my tears receive
And heal my wounds defil'd with noxious gore;
The punishments incurred by sin remit,
And mitigate the swift, sagacious eye
Of sacred justice, boundless in its view.
By thy pure law, dread evils constant flow,
Direct my steps, and pour Thy sacred light
In rich abundance on my clouded soul;
Dispel the dismal and malignant shades
Of darkness, pregnant with invenom's ills,
And to my body proper strength afford,
With health, whose pretence splendid gifts impart.
Give lasting fame; and may the sacred care …

A burning letter drops to the floor just after it stings my fingers, and I pick up the embers and the corner of the letter which are still intact.

I discard them in the sink on the pyre of yesterday's unwanted links and reminders, all the while waving the incense stick back and forth. Smoke from the burning letters and incense, and the solemn projection of the words from Proclus's hymn change the mood in the insanitary flat. Kenny remains where he sits and his leg is no longer twitching. The scent of the burning sage permeates the room and brings with it a transcendent cleansing.

> With which the fair-haired muses gifts, of old
> My pious ancestors preserved, be mine.
> Add, if it pleases thee, all-bestowing God,
> Enduring riches, piety's reward;
> For power omnipotent invests thy throne,
> With strength and universal rule.
> And if the whirling spindle of the fates
> Threats from the starry webs pernicion dire
> Thy shining shafts with force resistless send
> And vanguish 'ere it fall th' impending ill.

I run the cold water tap for several seconds on the smouldering remnants of the sacrificed links to the past. He stirs from his reverie and asks if I'd like a hand to clean up, and I say he doesn't need to worry about it and promise I'll leave everything just as I found it. There is only one part of the ritual to complete so I stand centrally, facing where he is sitting, holding the burning sage in one hand. The Roman candle is steady in the other:

> By the names *Adonai* and *Tetragrammaton* and *Jehovah* and by all the holy names I invoke the great spirit of the void. With the power of the holy names and the spirit of the void I break the link that ties Kenny P--- to the past. Through these flames the negative link of energy oppressing Kenny P--- is now broken. In the name of *Adonai, Yeshua* and *Tetragrammaton*, and *Jehovah*. Amen. Amen. Amen.

Something happened. Through a simple ritual we have changed the energy in his flat. Or at the very least we changed Kenny's interpretations of a series of historical facts weighing on his mind. And there is now more trust between us. The vibe is now more positive as we have got past the imbalance and tension which can fossilise between the outpatient or neurotic, and the workers supervising their care and rehabilitation.

Movements of the planets impact on the sun's magnetic field, and the alignment of certain planets are in symbiosis with unusual sunspot activity. All this touches life on earth to one extent or other, for if the planets have a bearing on the sun why wouldn't they have a bearing on earth? On the clearest night we might see up to three thousand stars, a fraction of the hundred billion stars that make up our galaxy. In deeper space are approximately ten billion similar galaxies. From these cosmic concatenations radiation is continually released. Sunspots and cosmic radiation are just two of many influences on our earth. In the purview of the cosmic configuration of the planets and the sun's significance to our earth, arcane devotion such as the *Hymn to the Sun* doesn't seem out of proportion.

A cultivated and protected professional distance guides the outpatient towards cooperation, compromise, and conformity. The patient is often reminded by mental health workers, some of whom they may genuinely like and trust, that their delusions or ideas have nothing to do with reality. The staunch consensus of disapproval is the stick in the carrot and stick analogy. If patients stay in the system long enough, they learn to control all words and gestures linked to fantastical thinking, delusions, grandiosity, and hallucination. Through hard experience they learn the fruit of their best thinking is not approved of by the professionals involved in their care. They learn Orwellian doublethink, a capacity to believe in two opposing points at the same time. They discover the skill of believing the reality their mind often presents them with, while at the same time fitting in with the actual reality reinforced by mental health workers.

They learn the tactical potency of words, since they cannot be criticised or punished for what they have not actually verbalised. Demons and visions, and sometimes comical grandiosities of confined and restricted minds in the empire of the mentally disordered, are our worst kept secrets. They prompt each other before ward rounds, case reviews, and community psychiatric assessments, reminding each other not to mention "you know what". The tighter the lid is kept on their delusions, the more the pressure of supervision is reduced. If they keep saying the right things at the right time in the presence of the right council of professionals, then it's another step towards freedom from the reach of the system. Denial of the fuller implications of mental disorder and a lack of trust in mental health workers is standard.

Kenny's trust has limits. He is wary of really opening up and speaking from the heart, because he has been a part of the system for so long, he would have surely gone through at least one breach of trust. It is not something I would have to search through his files for, or ask him directly. It has happened when he has confided in a staff member, and then what he said found its way back to the staff team to add yet more paranoia to how he sees those who have roles in caring for him.

Looked at from another angle, why should he trust any of us? In the reductive ways our lives are regulated, what could encourage us to think that any of us are doing anything outside our own personal interests? How many mortgages, foreign holidays, and car payment arrangements has his long involvement with mental health services helped finance? If the career development and financial rewards, humble as they often are compared with other sectors, were surgically incised from our work with Kenny, how many of us would bother going out of our way to help him? Naturally he doesn't trust us. Why should he?

But something shifted. He took in my every word and gesture during the ritual of fire and smoke from the incinerated photos and letters. The scent of sage has mesmerized him, at least for a minute or two. I can guess what he is thinking, for thoughts manifest on his expression as clearly as they can be carried on a string of words. If his psychiatrist or community psychiatric nurse knew what passed between us, they would have something to say on the matter. We have breached twin taboos, firstly by setting a fire in the home of a psychiatric outpatient with a conviction for arson. Secondly, we have strayed from the logic of our times by calling out to a source of inspiration in the great void outside our primary senses.

I drifted far enough from the norms to lose my job and Kenny understands this. The bond of trust between us solidifies as the power dynamics shift more in Kenny's favour, as he has now the option of having me sacked with just one phone-call. Quaint and old-fashioned concepts such as effective trade union representation and anything to do with employment rights do not exist out here in these killing fields of human morale. They might exist on paper but not in actuality. This fact is not lost on him. I know the actual symbolism of the ritual has touched him as I have never seen him sit up so watchfully and pay such attention.

We experimented with fire and it brought us into the heart of the moment. The experiment was significant in itself.

There is always a doubt with arsonists when mental disorder is linked to their fire-starting. They may really be troubled by the absence of one of the four key elements of air, fire, water, and earth. Through the millennia fire was the symbol of kinship and survival. With a climate like we have in the British Isles, our forefathers would not have survived without fire. Gathered around an evening fire, the flames and embers were surely an elixir for the psyche and an inspiration for the fables, yarns, and ghost stories which fanned early cultures into life. Sounding out disconnections with our past and gaps in our modern lives, the mentally disordered man or woman in crisis can be a rallying cry for a collective loss.

Over-sensitive minds and hearts are dismayed by the absence of ritual in our communal lives which the pace and necessity of modern life have wiped from our thoughts and memories. In a pragmatic submission to the gods of logic, doesn't it make more sense to feed the arsonist's hunger for the naked flame rather than starving it? Wouldn't an hour or so a few evenings a week staring into the flames of a fire lit in a brazier or surrounded and kept safe by stones make more sense? Are we innocent to believe that the state's mental health doctrines and the broader philosophy of psychiatry are concerned with integrating the mental health sufferer with the four basic elements, or reintroducing the cultural and tribal assurances of earlier ages?

Down here at this crossroads it feels like political and cultural dogma, part of a movement to globalise a glum, materialist, and reductive model of psychiatric diagnosis and care based on unrealistic notions of technologically driven progress. In its manifestations in the public sector, it erases all thoughts and references of beneficial outcomes of pyromaniacs staring into the flames of a controlled fire. Without much by way of compromise, it props up a cultural norm whereby oil-heated radiators have replaced open fires. It grinds on towards its own short-sighted and self-determined goals. Orthodoxies concede little time and space to criticisms at odds with their own fixed aims and values.

I clean up the mess I have created in Kenny's sink, take my roman candle and what remains of the stick of sage incense, and place them in a side-pocket of my rucksack. He is on his feet, animated and wanting to know if I think it will really work, if the words and smouldering fragments from the past will have any real effect in breaking links to his own past. I tell him about an experiment where a dozen patients were given medication while another dozen suffering from the same medical problem were given a placebo. The rate of recovery in the group who were given a placebo was higher than in the patients who had taken medication.

So often it's a question of will and belief. If we will something strongly enough, then it must manifest to one degree or other. If we believe a ritual invoking the sacred names of a deity has the power to break the loop of negative spiritual energy connecting us to the past, then something will happen. We are not helpless in influencing or changing our immediate encompassment. He didn't say anything by way of an answer. Maybe he was thinking about the times in the past when he did act in synch with his will and what the outcomes were. His flat is only about ten minutes away from the high street, so we agree to walk that way and take a coffee together in the most convenient coffee-shop. During our walk a new sense of comradeship lightens our steps. In his eyes maybe I am not so removed from his continuing reality as he thought. We are on foot, walking the streets of London together. We laugh at the absurdities of the day. Our problems and anxieties are not so very different.

Working closely with guys like Kenny, I find them to be unusually sensitive to the nuances and moods of others. It's as if through their suffering they have tapped into extrasensory perception regarding the motives and character of everyone they come into contact with. They are quick to pick up on ego, pride, selfishness, insincerity, and arrogance. In particular, they sense the vaguest trace of aloofness. Often they function in a default mode of survival, understanding that the system can never really help them with their most important health problems. They feed off emotional interactions with fellow patients and with the mental health workers they encounter. When we stay in the moment and experience our sensations and exchanges without trying to interpret what they might mean, much of the anxiety haunting our days and dreams can dissolve as if by magic.

We sit at a table outside one of the popular high street chains so that he can smoke. In a newspaper article earlier in the week the coffee-shop chain was criticised when samples of its coffee were found to contain traces of faecal matter. The pragmatist reads such things as a token of an overall imperfection, a sign of the fall, and drinks the coffee anyway. This is reality after all. It's not a utopia.

It's mid-morning so there is plenty of space at the tables. We watch the ebb and flow of the morning street, and he sucks on his roll-up and slurps from his cappuccino, leaving a ring of froth and chocolate powder around his top lip. He speaks freely about his life, about his parents and brother and two sisters, and about the most promising time in his early twenties before too much LSD and a series of hospitalisations in mental health wards in effect ruined his life.

His misery and dysfunction are tangled with family dynamics winding back through the generations. A subverted adolescence held back the necessary transitions from emotional dependence on his parents to the full psychosocial implications of young adulthood. This evolution was far more arduous than it ought to have been. He mentions that both his sisters suffer from bipolar disorder and various lesser maladies, both psychological and physical. They spend their most productive hours at home watching daytime television and overeating. It's an existence rather than a life. They are part of the millions perched on settees and couches soaking up endless television programmes, sedating the peripheries of a numbed consciousness. The programmes gently press home the stereotypes, vicarious living, and prejudices of a technologically driven, and also strange, prosperity.

His sisters watch the screen through medicated eyes, cigarettes in hand, consuming minutiae in the lives of others, while subliminally concluding that their own lives are not worth living. In this morass of endless screen-gazing and voyeurism, we still expect answers from our mental health system, and from cadres of time-harried mental health workers. It is almost like Kenny and so many others need a miracle every day in their lives just to keep going. And somehow if we understand miracles as scientific happenings not fully shaped into recognised formulas, the miracles do happen.

In the light of the complexity of Kenny's ailments, misery, and powerlessness, compounded by the misery and inertia of family members he has never managed to emotionally free himself from, we can only speculate as to what effect a humble ritual of fire and incense might have. The world seems a little tired today with the healing vibes that are on hand more scant when set beside the psychic vandalism of the age. So often the value of humanity is reduced to figures on a balance sheet or simply passed over in the ordinary hassle and indifference of another day. At times it is hard to see it at all.

With so many forces pressing on Kenny from so many angles, even old clichés such as "where there's life there's hope" are useful. My energy is waning and in my mind's eye I see a vista of solitude somewhere by the sea, with an old Victorian pier to one side and a lighthouse to the other. In solitude all is renewed and all is forgiven. I can almost taste the tang of sea air. Kenny says he has a whole ton of stuff he would like to burn ritually to cut more negative links to the past. I tell him we can get back to it another day. It can be our project, to keep going with the rituals until he feels the weight of negativity from the past lifting from his shoulders.

In rituals lasting several hours combined with meditation, fasting, input from enlightened souls, and hours of sitting around blazing fires in the company of the wise, so much could be improved. The aura of sadness and rage which loops so tightly about Kenny's etheric body could then be weakened, and in time chased away. But his care and support are tick-listed by managers who have never met him and his treatment follows on in the tradition of treatment for the pauper lunatics of an earlier century. Or, in other words, he cannot expect very much.

At least something hopeful has happened today and this happening beams a light on his horizons. I sense he feels a little more important and connected to a universal reality above and beyond the inquisitions from mental health nurses and psychiatrists he hates so much. Something happened. We implored the holy names for mercy and intervention. We fanned a vibe into life which lifted us out of the passing moments. It's a start, a nod in the right direction.

He wants to know if I'd like another coffee. I look at my watch and see that the hours have passed quickly. Then he wants to know if I can go with him to the shopping centre as there are a few small things he needs to buy. Bonds of trust have strengthened between us. The *Hymn to the Sun* and the aroma of sage linger as we speak. It's a more engaged man sitting on the other side of the coffee-shop table. The negative force which normally cocoons him is lessening. It's an overcast day but the sun appears from nowhere as if to thank us for honouring it with the words of Proclus. It blesses the moments with its immensity. Judging by how he is speaking and by the change in his posture and general movements, the *Hymn to the Sun* has eased some of the darkness damning his life and bringing him so much conflict and suffering. Who can say how long it will last?

I tell him I would love to go with him to the shops or sit a bit longer at the coffee-shop table, but I am already running late for the next appointment. He understands that time is a cold-eyed master with not much sympathy for the fuller hopes and yearnings of humankind. To admit to having free time or extra time at this crossroads of hyper-consumerism is to raise eyebrows. We shake hands, and new signs of hope take shape in how he looks out on the world. The more he believes rituals can help him, the more help he'll get from them. I walk to a nearby Overground train station to begin the day's next challenge, as the sun floods the street with incredible light.

I close my eyes for several seconds and hold my face upwards in thanks. For the remainder of the walk to the station there is a living connection between these earthly minutes and the sun. There are connections too between the sun and Proclus's solar homage. The simple ritual of fire in Kenny's flat is meaningful here in the sunshine. By side-stepping the killing touch of authority, we have actually got something done here today, whereas normally we get little if anything done. There is now a brighter light playing on Kenny's inner worlds of darkness.

On the short train journey my spirits dip and slide downwards to where all traces of the sun are absent. I am on my way to see Desmond. On a bad day his energy fields are a vortex into which the brightest thoughts of an entire day can disappear in seconds. Desmond is of a greater concern to the mental health system, as he has taken a human life. They downgraded the charge from murder to manslaughter and sent him to a high-security hospital for the criminally insane, where he served eleven years in a locked ward. In fairness it was all a long time ago. It's a different Desmond walking the earth now.

If there's anyone in the history of the esoteric who needs a little love for their drive to improve their knowledge, it must be Pythagoras. Daniel and Ezekiel initiated him into the mysteries of the Cabala but only after he forfeited his foreskin in a ritual of circumcision. After many trials of character in Egypt, the secrets of the priesthood were revealed to him by special permission of King Amasis. One of the noble precepts of Pythagorean thought is:

> There is no evil which is not to be preferred before anarchy.

The good sense of this statement comes to life for some moments in my thoughts, and I value those seekers who have gone before us. What is viewed as evil lives with us in the banality of ordinary days as much as in the raging eddies of demonology and in the intrigue and hatred between nations. On meeting Desmond for the first time Pythagoras's point is a beam of awareness, a forewarning of the percentage of men born for anarchy. There are men who love anarchy so that they can act out more fully on earth the demonic energies raging inside them.

Again, it is not a view valued by our psychiatric hegemony. It is not an idea I would try to explain to colleagues or to my line manager or to NHS mental health workers. We do not see or hear demons and we do not speak of them. They are dangerous delusions suffered by patients. We must do all we can to reassure the patient that demons are only delusions and that they have no significance or meaning other than as a symptom of mental illness. Yet when I think of Desmond, this is the first idea to take up space in my mind. It's a binding thought association. Desmond—demons.

Cultural values and norms of any age frame medical and psychiatric approaches to mental disorder. Not one given the help of a cure stands outside the influences of the society and culture it is part of. In the pagan and early pagan-Christian British Isles, talk of demons and magic was as prevalent as the discussions we hear today about climate change. It was an everyday discourse and found its way into both everyday and medical attitudes towards the mentally disordered.

When Augustine and his party of forty Christian missionaries arrived at Thanet in AD 597, Ethelbert the heathen king of Kent ordered them not to move off Thanet. The king insisted on meeting the monks in the open air, in the presence of the sky-king god. Once Ethelbert was satisfied that the monks could not call up demons and were not magicians, he allowed them to move off Thanet and preach to the people of Kent.

Western psychiatric methodology recreates madness in the image of its diagnostic models. On many levels it is busy helping to wipe out what little remains of folk cures, herbal wisdom, superstition, and natural medicine, while expanding the psychopharmacology project worldwide. Our psychiatric models of care point to chemical origins in mental disorder, and to cognitive distortion or damage as the salient tribulation. They encourage economically dependent nations to replace cultural and tribal definitions of disease and mental disorder with an all-encompassing devotion to the gods of psychopharmacology. Only a devotion, where ancestral beliefs and nature medicines are shunned as dangerous and outdated, is given a nod from on high. Only absolute belief in the charms and spells of western psychiatry legitimises the better placebo outcome. Only where there are no alternatives to psychiatric medicine is psychiatric medicine graced with the required power over everything.

If indeed we are now spreading the spiritual short-sightedness of our mental health system globally, then humankind in its totality must prepare itself for an Armageddon of sorrow, depression, and misfortune not experienced since the Great Plague. The cheap trick behind psychopharmacology's appetite for globalising mental health is an article of faith for the psychiatrist grounded in biology and brain-science research. It is dogma centring mental illness in the brain. Consequently, legions of scientific researchers prod and poke at the brains of laboratory animals. They chart chemical changes with scans of the human brain and revere the most up-to-date revelations of biology just like their forefathers revered the simples and cures blessed in the name of the Messiah and a host of saints, and before that followed the old pagan ways.

If the malaise really is subsumed in the workings of the biological brain, then such workings can be altered by medication. Hence the principle of medication is lifted even higher as the holiest diagnostic method. One outcome is that the profits of pharmaceutical companies rise and rise and the status of western psychiatry increases. It is all very persuasive when pieced together. Who could possibly argue against it?

Yet strange whispers are heard in our dreams, warning that the gods of psychopharmacology are not gods at all but rather demons with little to offer except the worshipping of money and ego, pointing the way to all the wrong turnings. It's the venture capitalists' wet dream after all, to make billions of dollars' profit from the false idea of mental disorder centred in the brain and only curable by drugs that oversee the brain's chemical processes. Reductive as it might seem, it is the basic model our psychiatric hierarchy insists on. It is the model we throwaway minions in the mental health infantry must measure up to. NHS recovery workers and support workers, and we lowly mental health charity workers, understand from our first day's employment that there is only one real mortal sin we can commit. And this sin is to say or do anything to interfere with the medication given to patients. We must join in the chorus when the patient is coerced, cajoled, enticed, or at times physically forced to take medication, notwithstanding the anguish it brings with it or its sometimes fatal side-effects. The consumption of medication is always fixed as the number one priority.

There is no sympathetic listening ear or mercy for anyone who raises doubts regarding whether the medication is doing any good for the mental overall health of the patient. To suggest a lower dose, a higher dose or another kind of medication is okay. Thousands of hours each year are frittered away in discussion by the psychiatric profession and its ancillary services in quarrels and long-winded team handovers to do with medication. But to support a patient by proposing that medication is not helping at all is taboo. To suggest a patient would be better off not taking any anti-psychotic medication is unthinkable. If the idealist frontline worker persists with this general opinion, they would find their presence in the sector criticised, questioned, and ultimately not wanted.

Again, as soon as Desmond enters my thoughts, I get the impression of demons. At this point it might be worth asking if demons are real. Maybe we can accept they are real in the sense that they at least exist in our minds. In given conditions our minds can regurgitate their images and some impressions linked to them. They also exist as a metaphor for the addictions and distractions that people must often deal with when they are not in control of their minds.

The suggestible personality is vulnerable to fads and mental disturbances. They might join a religious sect one week, but the next week leave to join a political group with a divisive agenda. Soon after they are overcome by the forceful personality of someone they have just met, and off they go again on another mission or crusade. In a sense the mind not under control of the will is a mind open to demons. But demons exist in actual spatial reality too, or in a complexity of spatial realities. The materialist philosophy behind the science movement tells us that this is untrue. But in our heart of hearts, in the still of night with the stars a heavenly halo around our thoughts, do we really believe that materialist thinking?

There is a tradition in Western magic that signs off the best outcomes of invocation, ritual, and conjuration to the wondrous and mostly hidden workings of the human mind. Yet in the magical traditions of many other lands demons are simply demons. They are real spatial entities. They are described by many who experience them in terms lucid enough to make the average state psychiatrist with neo-Darwinian leanings blanch. Faced with cultural evidence of the existence of demons, or jinns in the Arabic world, The Royal College of Psychiatrists simply sidesteps the question. On one of their official blogs, an RCPsych psychiatrist writes:

> I learned that it is best to resist the temptation to advocate a certain explanatory model of mental illness to collude or collide with cultural beliefs.

In a diagram the psychiatrist in question traces the symptoms of mental pathology back to neurotransmitters, transporters, and biochemical mechanisms. It is all a question of underlying factors and the temperament of the patient. Down at the very end of the line are the natural and supernatural causal factors and the patient's openness to reacting to such factors. In a neat sidestep, the spiritual beliefs of entire cultures are avoided as mainstream psychiatry points to chemical irregularities in the brain as the primary problem.

There is hardly a place in the world not influenced by these more reductive codes of Western science where demons, demon possession, and the casting out of demons are not understood and incorporated into cultural norms and logic. To this day in India demons are purged from their victims by shamans known as *babas*. In John Stanley's noteworthy studies into the healing work by *babas* in Pune, he emphasised how none of those subject to exorcism were aware of any physical pain. The agonies and writhing about were endured only by the demon. Stanley discovered that the people troubled by demons were brought back to normal health or their health was improved by the healing method in question.

Cultural and cosmic systems are now under the scrutiny of the jealous eye of a globally motivated psychiatry. This disbelieving eye waits patiently for more opportunities to dissect mental disorder from its cultural and cosmic relationship and to centre it in the chemistry of the brain. With the overall template of mental health work in mind, what hope does the humble charity mental health worker on the doorsteps of despair have of making sense of a word association where the name Desmond equates to demons?

He is slow to answer the door of his flat. I know he is in there and that he will get around to answering the doorbell in his own time. He is playing *Queen's Greatest Hits* at quite a high volume. As I wait, I wonder if his neighbours value his taste in music or, if they don't, they at least tolerate it. It's the middle of the day and the noise from passing buses and trucks is deafening, so loud music is not inexcusable. Because of his life-changing index offence, He knows that his supervision can often feel like he is on the end of a forensic gaze. His flat is a goldfish bowl where little goes unnoticed. I can hear him calling out above the music, telling me to hang on a minute. He took an innocent life with appalling violence, and how he went about it would upset most people. I hope you will excuse me if for the sake of confidentiality I don't talk about the details here, as even the simplest outline of his crime would give away his identity. He finally opens the door and sticks out a fat, moist hand in welcome, and I shake the hand once bloodied by human slaughter years before.

The former Catholic priest and authority on demons Francis McNutt differentiates between what he describes as true demons from hell, which he considers to be quite rare, and other cases where people are troubled or oppressed by demons. McNutt views many mentally ill people as oppressed by spirits, and as a result "demonised" is a word he is happy to use. These earthbound spirits can cause serious psychic harm, often not on purpose. McNutt's views are not unheard of in psychiatry. The psychiatrists Dr Ralph Allison, Dr M Scott Peck (author of *The Road Less Travelled*) and Dr Carl Wickland have identified and written about demon possession in their patients. To one degree or other their interventions accepted the influence or presence of demons in mental disorder.

A Yoruba friend once spoke of a busy marketplace in the town he was born and brought up in and said it was nearly always busy, but that those who went there were not always human. I thought it was a kind of pun. Or maybe he was talking about livestock or pets moving about the human throngs? But no, he literally meant what he said. He meant a number of those wandering past the busy market stalls appeared to be ordinary Yoruba people, but with a second glance the observer could see they were not human at all. To the European mind this is quite a statement. Not human at all? They are actually dead my friend explained. But they're not aware that they are dead. Their etheric bodies have not yet left this plane. Some of them have very personalised reasons why they haven't departed this place at death, important bonds still unifying their spirits with the world of the living. Others were used by juju practitioners for cunning reasons, their bodies preserved and unburied, waiting for the spirit to re-enter the flesh it had once known as its own.

The image magnified into mental vividness, a marketplace buzzing with commerce and strong voices haggling over the best price. We can almost feel the sun, immense like the god of ages, and see inhuman shapes meandering past the stalls and wares as they often did when they were alive. The collective life of a people is strengthened by such frames of reference, with bonds of kinship endorsed by knowledge alien to outsiders. My friend's casual remark has real implications for the spiritual and tribal identity of the Yoruba. All of them are not human.

Keeping an open mind, I asked others about the likelihood of an inhuman presence in the marketplace, probing for a metaphor or fable with a transcendent cultural truth. I was reassured that it was not a symbol or a story told at bedtime, nor was it a way of commenting on groups of people living in the bush. It was the truth in literal terms. Either those in question were alive and possessed by spirits, or they were dead with their life-forms animated by spirits, sometimes guided from the world of the dead to the living by juju practitioners.

The Africans I spoke with were polite and helpful but reserved too. They were wary of talking about too many of the finer points of life in their homeland and about sightings of inhuman spirits in the marketplace. At times they seemed a little embarrassed by the topic, or unconvinced that it was a subject they should be discussing with a European at all. This is the land of logic after all, a land where citizens can legally be locked away and medicated for verbalising what is culturally accepted as delusional in European eyes. Understandably the matter of inhuman manifestation in marketplaces is not an easy one. I asked the same question of a matriarch from a family of Igbo healers. She explained that the marketplace spirits are real, most likely the result of several different processes or events. It's not necessarily one universal phenomenon bringing them to the marketplace. It is a real fear in Africa she said, that people's spirits will not find peace after death. It's a real fear that they will wander the nights in a reality between life and death because of a negative intervention from ancestors or tribal deities.

The rational mind pauses here. Bearing in mind the everyday fields of perception most of us are familiar with, is it within reasonable limits to believe in non-human apparitions? In a post-colonial summary, there are other discourses. Fear of change is a factor in African interpretations of the world. The marketplace represents change and the African struggle with a rapid rate of social change can retreat to a more familiar and reassuring reference point. Fear of change can be likened to tribal, Biblical, or Koranic notions of evil. The marketplace becomes a symbol for a much-feared change which must be evil or demonic. Non-human spectres wandering through the busy market-stalls are really the projected fears of people fearful of a discomforting pace of change. They only see a personification of their own fears. Or do they?

We don't generally see spectres or non-human persons wandering about marketplaces, in Africa or here or anywhere. Only when the sensual references are expanded are such visions in any way possible. Or there may really be a few people with clairvoyant skills, who can see or hear impressions the rest of us cannot. As a philosopher of note once said, what we don't understand we must pass over in silence. As unfamiliar as all this might sound, it forms part of a holistic approach and must at least be given some consideration.

My mind cannot help drifting away in less charted directions, when I am anywhere close to Desmond. It is harder not to think about the recorded sightings and influences of demons and earthbound spirits, and to ponder the universal correlation between certain mental disorders and demon possession. He told me in the past that he occasionally sees the devil. As far as I am aware, the answer from his forensic psychiatrist is always in terms of medication. He has already gone past the recommended levels of his anti-psychotic medication, and the side-effects leave him tired and hungry. He overeats and is grossly obese.

He is dystonic and his tongue often sticks out of his mouth in a ludicrous way. Weight gain through the long-term use of clozapine can be alarming. It's not unusual for mental health patients to gain sixty or ninety pounds on this anti-psychotic medication. Patients can die from its drastic effects on the metabolism, or from its propensity to kill white blood cells. Patients prescribed clozapine must have their white blood cells monitored closely, with monthly, fortnightly, or weekly visits to the bloods clinic of a local hospital. When death comes through clozapine, it often comes through a stroke.

Constipation and inflammation in the bowels are other not uncommon side-effects of the drug. Patients die from toxic mega-colon. The anti-psychotic blocks the serotonin receptors as well as the acetyl choline muscarinic receptors. A dilated colon, severe constipation, ischaemic necrosis, and a perforated bowel can be caused by clozapine. The anti-psychotic meds can literally poison the bowels of those who ingest them.

Tricyclic antidepressants and anti-cholinergic drugs to counter the side-effects of hypersalivation when combined with clozapine increase the likelihood of deterioration in bowel health and constipation. The post-psychotic patient dealing with the wreckage of a life devastated by mental breakdown must also have their colon and intestines poisoned by psychopharmaceutical medication. In the worst-case scenario, one day they will find that they are just about coping with severe constipation, and out of the blue their pulse and blood-pressure will plummet. They might pass out and someone will call for an ambulance. The paramedics who show up will find a high level of oxygen saturations. Oxygen will be applied. The patient will go into cardiac arrest. Attempts to revive them will fail. Unfortunately, the cure can also kill. Another failure of the culture of deinstitutionalisation is that tens of thousands of post-psychotic outpatients are left alone in flats and rented rooms even when their medication, if not administered correctly, has serious repercussions for their health. There is nobody around to monitor medication or to work out when it is time for a medication review. A percentage of outpatients are given outreach workers who visit from time to time.

The emergency services are generally left to pick up the pieces of the failures of deinstitutionalisation. How they must hate the very mention of the term, which is so often a euphemism for wishful thinking. Selling off the old asylums to property developers, so that they could be converted into golf courses and homes fit for the very wealthy, satisfied certain political appetites. But the outcomes are momentous, shifting the burden of care from state psychiatry to ordinary people with enough worries of their own and to police officers and paramedics. Perhaps the policy of deinstitutionalisation will one day be fully documented and viewed in a broader picture of its successes and failings.

We might be naïve in still calling for more egalitarianism in a world where tiny percentages of the population dominate every stratum of commerce, wealth ownership, creative industry, and opportunity. But the abject misery of everyday mental health work is largely balanced on the head of a psychological meltdown caused by hopeless odds in the game of life. And the only option for those playing a game that cannot be won is to opt out entirely.

We sit in Desmond's tidy front room where the greatest hits of Queen are still playing on the stereo, but at a much lower volume. I have several pieces of work to sort out on his behalf, so I get straight to it and ring the local council to follow up on his Freedom Pass renewal application.

He is anxious about it, even though I have assured him more than once that it is all routine. There is no reason why the pass should not be renewed. I know it is crucial as it gives him free travel throughout London's public transport system, but his anxiety is disproportionate in much the same way that every aspect of his existence in the world is disproportionate.

I am meant to take him out today, to go with him to a mental health daycentre about a twenty-minute bus ride away, but he says he's too tired to go. It's understandable. Clozapine blues. As soon as I leave, he will turn up the volume on *Queen's Greatest Hits* and curl up on the settee to sleep the sleep of medicated oblivion for what remains of the afternoon. A large-screen television commands one wall of the sitting-room, and to one side dvds are stacked to a precarious height.

The films are of the Hollywood blockbuster genre. He likes superhero films: *X-Men* is his current favourite. He spends the evenings watching television and dvds, and enjoys takeaway food. In the past I have brought several diet plans and recipes for simple, cheap, and healthy meals, but he showed no interest in them. Another former mental health patient who he met in hospital visits now and then, as he lives not far away. This visitor battered a hapless pensioner he didn't know to death with a brick, and he and Desmond get on famously. Desmond speaks to a few people at the mental health daycentre he visits but mostly he is on his own. If the side-effects of clozapine don't kill him then loneliness and social isolation probably will.

In one of the residential mental health projects where I worked, the staff were hyper-alert when dealing with meds for fear of touching clozapine tablets. I too fell into line with the practice whereby all skin contact with the clozapine pills was avoided. None of us wanted to risk touching tablets known to be poisonous. We were told the pills could damage our white blood cells. Yet the mental health patients in our care consumed them daily and at a high volume.

Desmond is tired, although he hasn't done much today, or on any day really. His puffy eyelids are already closing, and he yawns like one of the perpetually bored lions at London Zoo. I finish up the phone-calls and assure him all his paperwork is up to date. The relevant council department will post his Freedom Pass in the next week or two. There is one outstanding questionnaire we are obliged to fill in but he is too tired to answer the questions spewed out by yet another government computer. His chemically numbed brain, never the sparkiest at the best of times, is dulling and closing down on the verges of yet more sleep. The bureaucracy must wait for another day.

On a shelf a crucifix and an inspirational picture of Jesus in a pound shop silver frame are reminders of his occasional visits to a local church. The question is begging to be asked, but with the prevailing orthodoxy in mind dare I ask it? Our medicos and senior managers in the public sector have sacrificed Desmond to the Pythagorean principle whereby any evil is preferable to anarchy. An unmedicated Desmond is an incarnation of anarchy from the Dark Ages. Scars on his knuckles and defiance in his eyes are conspicuous after years of incarceration, medication, and correction. They are mementoes of a primary rage, the same rage which hurried him into the care of the state in the first place.

Having discussed Desmond's index offence with him several times, my thoughts drift again to the conclusion that he was cajoled or tormented by evil spirits at the time. Based on everything I know about him, it is the only sane conclusion. He comes across as highly predisposed to impressions, impulses, and energies from other people, and could be described as remarkably impressionable. If his personality is so easily swayed by the personalities of others, then is it unthinkable that he is just as open to discarnate influences?

His occasional sightings of the devil and his other visions are always quickly closed down by the forensic psychiatrist managing his care. He is prevented from speaking of them or referring to them in anything other than the shortest sentence or two. It is not that his negative visions have stopped troubling him, but more how he has stopped mentioning them to his psychiatrist and community mental health nurse. He knows by now that descriptions of his visions are not what they want to hear and only mentions them half-heartedly. In mentioning them he is taking a chance that I am not the kind of person to ring his clinical team as soon as I get back to the office to report what he said.

The demons troubling Desmond do not fit easily into the category of demons from hell that the former Catholic priest Francis McNutt believes are extremely rare. They are more the kind of demons troubling or oppressing a small percentage of people, the "demonised" as McNutt describes them. But I have seen him having a bad week, as he calls it, and during these bad weeks he showed the symptoms of possession as described by McNutt and by John Stanley in his studies of the *baba* healers of Pune.

Only the intervention of a visionary psychiatrist could possibly steer the narrative towards the conclusion that Desmond is practically screaming out for spiritual healing. And it would take the steely, coordinated will of his clinical team together with lots of imagination to try something other than paralysing his mind with clozapine and reducing him to a docile couch potato who listens to *Queen's Greatest Hits* on repeat. In the absence of visionary psychiatrists and the focused will of mental health teams, his treatment must go on much as before.

With Desmond our lips are sealed. There is nothing to do or say. His forensic history makes it impossible to add anything or to suggest a more holistic conceptualisation of his care and treatment. As a lowly mental health worker, they would laugh at me. I would be lucky not to get sent back to my agency, P45 in hand. Art, poetry, spirituality, and creativity in general are luxuries around here. In the Anglican church Desmond sometimes goes to, the vicar waves off the rites of exorcism as an anachronism, yet coincidently the image of St. Dunstan gripping the devil by the nose with red-hot pincers is immortalised in the church's stained glass windows. In Christian records Dunstan has numerous encounters with the devil, including a quarrel that ends in the scene depicted above. Saint Dunstan and Desmond would have so much to talk about.

In the suspected demonic possession of the American boy David Glatzel, the main reason his mother Judy turned down the option of exorcism was because of what she saw as too many rules. Her local priests had to run through a psychological assessment with her. She had taken her son to a Bridgeport psychiatrist who had charged her an exorbitant hourly rate and then announced that he needed the input of all the family in a series of related clinical sessions. The church authorities were legally coerced to fall into line with psychiatric propriety. They could not begin an exorcism until the church, the boy, and the boy's family complied with statutory psychiatric standards, examinations, and procedures. Judy Glatzel finally withdrew her son from the pre-exorcism psychological assessments, disheartened by what she saw as a tepid church response:

> They just want to stick needles in my kid. There's no way in hell they're going to do that ... If people honestly believe in Jesus Christ our Lord, they have to believe in the devil.

For those who went before us, judicial torture and witch-pricking were accepted as part of due legal process. The association of these institutional outrages with the persecution of the defenceless, poor, and mentally disordered, and present-day attempts at exorcism, is fixed in our collective consciousness. The malicious workings of the Inquisition in searching for the devil's mark on their unfortunate victims poisoned the European mind to all mention of spirits and demon possession. The torture, drownings, legalised theft of property, burning at the stake, and purging of what were alleged to be harmful spirits amount to an imposition on the sensitivities of the European mind on a par with the totalitarian outrages of the early and mid-twentieth century.

The psychic wound cuts deep to this day. The very mention of spirit possession as a factor in cases of mental disorder is enough to stir deep emotions. The response of the modern rationalist is a pointed reminder of how mental health has moved on since the days when we burnt people alive as witches, when they may well have been suffering from mental disorder. In the light of this collective psychic wound, the caution of present-day churches is understandable. The more accepted and respectable the Western church is, the slower it is to begin the rites of exorcism. Western orthodoxy is now tempered by a culture of psychiatry and its associated disciplines, which shadows all spheres of belief and faith.

To hold onto ancient privileges, the established Churches must bow to the secular gods of Freud, Skinner, Klein, Adler, et al. Smaller and more independent denominations have a broader canvas on which to work. Pentecostal churches especially hold a defiant and energetic position on demonic possession, an attitude very much at odds with the secular rationality of Western orthodoxy. I was curious about how they see such things, interested in how they might behold a man like Desmond, and whether they would judge him to have a disposition to demons.

Keeping as open a mind as possible, I set out to look more closely into how demons are dealt with in Pentecostalism. As a Londoner, I already had an advantage, as the Pentecostal ministries in the greater metropolitan area are many and varied. My esoteric Christian instincts can adapt to any interpretations of the deity within reason, so the investigation began cheerfully enough. There was little learnt during my initial inquiries. Congregations I contacted were mostly of a European identity and were reserved and at times quite cagey on all questions of worship and spirit possession. They referred all such questions to the scriptures or to their central office. The arcane heart does not take easily to such religious literalism, so these conversations did not go anywhere at all. A pastor with halitosis lectured me in a draughty hallway and I knew he didn't trust me or want me to hang around for long, with our energy fields antagonistically oppositional. In truth I found out nothing at all about demon possession.

Congregations with a more diverse ethnic make-up and with non-European pastors were more interesting. Inside makeshift church halls in Lambeth, Southwark, and Merton, people were seemingly touched and moved by spirits. Elders proudly told me that the worshippers in rapture were possessed by the Holy Spirit, enchanted, with rolling eyes and waving arms. Several had fallen backwards only to be caught by church wardens and elders. Others were talking in tongues, or, if you like, babbling inanely. Elders were clearly uncomfortable when I hung around for longer than a few minutes. Or maybe I flatter myself, as looking back it seems the entire congregation was uncomfortable with me hanging around for any length of time at all.

At a church in one of the poorest boroughs in London, the swooning, fainting, eye-rolling, and shrieking involved almost everyone present. The pastor and his elders went from worshipper to worshipper, seemingly purging them of demons or confirming the descent of the Holy Spirit. A vibe close to hysteria electrified the low-ceilinged, rectangular room of the main worshipping space. Windows were covered by drawn blinds, and one man began running around the limits of the room with his face twisted by pain or ecstasy, lapping the room repeatedly, a lone runner at a gathering of moaning, eye-rolling supplicants. I had a feeling the pastor and his elders would try to rope me into the orgy of possession.

At a glance it was obvious that they were men with dominant, somewhat aggressive personalities, and were not going to allow a stranger to stand with them, as they went through their theatrical contortions and fainting fits. I visualised a blue luminous pentagram and closed my eyes to increase the potency of the visualisation, projecting thoughts into the minds of the pastor and his elders moving past the swooning, moaning believers. They were getting closer to where I stood alone and at a slight distance from the others. It is an effective but underrated technique of defence, to project focused streams of thought into the mind or minds of those who may not have our best interests at heart.

If people work at it, and increase their powers of concentration, they would be surprised at the outcomes. Through the practice of meditation and thought-control, almost anyone can learn to hold a fixed idea in their mind, and once a fixed idea is projected through mental energy, the results are nearly always interesting.

The pastor and his elders walked by me without a glance, their thought-waves interrupted by mental energy sent towards them. It is based on a simple principle, like the trick of avoiding eye-contact with troublemakers in the street or on public transport. Without eye-contact it is difficult if not impossible for a disturbed or criminally minded stranger to attack. In the Pentecostal church the dominating pastor and elders could not walk up to me directly. Their wills were deflected by my will in a mental energy variation of the rabbit caught in headlights.

I looked around, reviewing in my mind the cases of suspected possession I had read about, where the church had insisted on psychological assessment before rites of exorcism. In the low-ceilinged room filled with fainting, gibbering worshippers, the idea of a psychological or psychiatric screening prior to demon-purging rituals seemed rational and necessary. Some of the congregation caught up in the fainting and swooning were familiar. I had come across them in my work in mental health. They could be categorised as vulnerable adults and you might meet them in mental health daycentres or find them drying an anorak on the heaters of a local library or queuing at foodbanks.

They are often out on a limb culturally too, cut off from a truer sense of identity, family, community, ancestors, and kinship ties in faraway post-colonial lands. They are thrown into the sink-or-swim trials of an impersonal European capital and world centre of indifference. I have spoken with them at length and walked beside them for a while on their transitional journeys. Now I stood with them in a Pentecostal church as they gave themselves heart and soul to the pushy, ambitious personalities of money-concerned ministers and elders. At least in the claustrophobic room of worship, flanked on one side by a kebab takeaway and on the other side by yet another boarded-up shop, they were somebody. They existed as human beings and were important enough for an entity as exalted as the Holy Spirit to enter them, or at least they were important enough for the pastor to insist that the Holy Spirit had entered them. For an hour or two they had escaped impersonality and their low-status existence in an often unfriendly European city, where they are mostly invisible, misunderstood, monitored by security cameras, or seen as outsiders.

They sang, danced, and clapped their hands, and when the minister and the elders stood in front of them to proclaim that the Holy Spirit had entered them, they rolled their eyes, swooned, and fainted on cue. They were caught by strong hands, and then lowered safely to the ground, unified with a higher conception of existence, as powers in their subliminal minds were unleashed in spasms of wild energy. Up at the front of the room, the minister and his elders reconvened. They rolled up their sleeves and got down to the serious business of healing the afflicted, including banishing demons from a shy woman pressed forward by the willing hands of several others. Nobody in their right mind would bring Desmond to such a service. The emotions pricked into life by the minister and his elders are peculiar to a given cultural experience of a displaced people, a diaspora reclaiming their human identity in the practised impersonality of an impersonal European city.

It was an intimate ritual of belonging, and I was an outsider among outsiders, an intruder at events, which were only what we could call religious or Christian in the abstract. I drifted down the room, until I disappeared into the shadows close by the exit-door. There was a great wail from the front where the uncertain woman who had stepped forward for healing had fallen back into the arms of her supporters. The minister was exhorting and shouting with the fullness of his tenor-bass voice. I had intruded long enough into the intimacy of a business I have no real business intruding on, so I quietly stepped out unnoticed into the welcoming evening breezes. It was useful as nearly all such scenarios have significance when taking a holistic approach to psychological and psychiatric disorders and the suffering they bring in their wake.

What was eye-opening at these Pentecostal services was not just the vulnerability of most of those present but the fact that there was evidence of spirit possession in many of those who had showed up. But it was not as the ministers and elders claimed: a descent of the Holy Spirit. It was something far more banal and more common than this. They were opening up their astral bodies to whatever spirit essences were in the air at the time. As a result, they were attracting the energies of astral-shells and earth-bound spirits. They were indeed possessed, but not in a very potent sense, and not by the Holy Spirit. They were troubled and niggled by lower forms of spiritual energies. These energies are categorised by Francis McNutt as different from demons from hell. Most of the Pentecostal services were directed in such a way. The participants, often vulnerable, alienated, and with the usual unresolved psychosocial impediments all too common to the human condition, were encouraged to let go of their inhibitions and defences. They opened themselves up to earthbound spirits or spiritual influences from the Astral Plane.

They put themselves in danger and then allowed the ministers and elders to shout and shock them back to a functioning level of normality, purely by the strength of more dominant personalities. They were not possessed by a malignant or hellish demon as such and then healed by the Holy Spirit through the special intervention of the ministers or elders. Instead, they had opened themselves up to earth-bound spiritual influences, which were then dissipated by the overbearing personalities of the Pentecostal ministers and elders. The Holy Spirit had not descended.

They had attracted the troubled spirits of dead people, many of whom who were not even aware they were dead, as they were trapped in astral shells. Or they had connected in a tangential way with energy from the Astral Plane. The lack of sympathy with the frailty of the human spirit and the boorishness of the ministers and elders were unsettling. They were either blindly ignorant or, if they knew what they were doing, were mean and scheming.

Nothing I had seen should have surprised me. Pentecostal churches throughout the world are investigated by authorities with wearying consistency. Perversely it is nearly always to do with a pointless love of cheap materialism. In the West African city of Accra, the fetish priest Nana Kwaku Bonsam brought a legal case against a Pentecostal minister who had hired him to bring down the gods of the Ashanti in his favour. But the Pentecostal minister had then not paid the agreed price. During a legal hearing, eyebrows were raised as to why a Christian Pentecostal minister had paid for the services of a fetish priest in the first place.

It is common, Nana Kwaku Bonsam explained, for Pentecostal ministers to pay for fetish priests to conjure native gods in the hope of favours, especially when they are in the early stages of building up their church numbers. These strange assemblies are not typical of Christian healing in its broadest context, and it is wrong to mention them in the same breath as genuine Christian healers such as the Ethiopian Orthodox Church's Memhir Girma. They are the last places on earth where someone with Desmond's problems should show up, but where exactly it is possible for him to show up? Even holistic approaches have their limits.

He falls asleep momentarily in front of me and then wakes with a start and apologises. He is fearful of his demonic visions, fearful too of the forensic psychiatrist and community mental health team who marshal his visions into a more acceptable translation. Fear motivates him, animates his days, and haunts his nights. I say I must go. There will be other appointments where we can work on the outstanding paperwork. Some time in the future maybe there will be hope of purging his etheric body and his astral body of demonic elements. I do not know exactly what draws negative spirits to him or what exact event in his life or in a previous life is the key to it all.

There will not be time to look more closely at the source of his malaise through regression therapy or rituals of healing or exorcism. The gods of secular psychiatry and psychopharmacology have already marked out the terms of his condition, and endless political interfering in state health services compounds his bondage. On top of that, this is the age of the hyper-consumerist, the secularist, and the technocrat who are forever in a hurry, so there just isn't time. There isn't time for very much beyond the usual masquerade.

There is always a cipher to decode, a clue which leads on to further clues. With one complex-needs adult it was hard not to notice a design tattooed in black ink high on her chest-bone. I don't know much about such things, but I knew enough at that time to recognise the work of a West African fetish priest. I asked her about it and she quickly buttoned up her summer blouse. She said that she and her two sisters were very sick as children, and that their mother asked for the help of a native healer. The healer tattooed her and conjured healing spirits, and she survived but both her sisters died. And the cost of the fetish-priest's intervention? She had spent her entire adult life in a haze of alcohol and drug addiction, sometimes homeless and nearly always under the gaze of the police and what mental health services are still out there. There may be connections: who can really say? Taking the longer view, there is usually a cipher, a clue leading to further clues.

On the Overground train back to the office I try to read a page or two from a psychology book, a tome on Gestalt counselling integrated with transactional analysis and psychosynthesis. The words swim senselessly in front of my eyes, and I cannot take anything in. The process had begun months before when the books on both conventional and radical psychology began losing their hold on my imagination. Increasingly they fell short of any kind of true bearing on the question of human development, mental disorder, and the wider philosophical dilemmas of mind. It was like watching the most glorious sunset in the history of humankind through a monochrome monitor only a few inches wide.

The more pages of psychology I flipped, the more my mind and spirit begged for connections with a deeper personal awareness, and with the majesty of nature. The page ended when the experimentalist arrives at a stark therapeutic moment where there is a choosing and rejecting of possibilities and overcoming obstacles. Then a whole new page opens where action in the world overcomes neurosis, where therapy ends and the work of raising true awareness begins. I don't know how much of it was conscious or if I was just overtired. But I left the book behind me on the train and I can't honestly say that I've missed it.

Eddie

I wake with a shout. It's just after three in the morning and the bedroom is unusually hot, even though it's a cold night. I dreamt lucidly about Tina. Or I should say it began as a dream and spiralled into a nightmare. The word she said, or I imagined she said, resounds in my semi-somnolent mind. She simply said the name of the part of London she was born and brought up in, and I heard the Kabbalistic word for Satan. I am trying to work out if it's my imagination or if by some weird coincidence, not at once understandable, she really said the word in question. I can't decide either way. The devil is addiction. Addiction is the devil. Why should it surprise me to hear the word on her lips?

It's a remarkably clear night and the stars are a balm for the senses. On the clearest night in the history of humankind, when the stars are most visible, what we can see of them is but a small fraction of what is actually out there. What must the stars look like in their totality and what do they really mean for us? As we flounder in reductive logic and mechanistic views, we are perplexed by wonder after wonder in a universe of stunning wonders. On certain nights it is as if the stars are looking down on us in mute pity.

A famous cosmologist has just rejected his fellow cosmologists' idea of the multiverse, the theory that there are numerous universes with their own laws of physics. Instead, he explains a new concept, the universe as a hologram. In this theorem the three-dimensionality of reality is an illusion, a hologram. There is no noticeable sign of humility here, of accepting that we cannot understand the mind of an unknowable God, and that there are things we are simply not meant to understand through logic alone. The cosmologists' speculations inspire a thought association like the thought association linking Desmond to the concept of demons. The thought association links contemporary cosmology with the idea of people whistling in the dark to keep up their spirits.

It is a struggle to get back to sleep, what with the immensity of the stars and the shock of seeing Tina so vividly in my dream. Like most dreams the narrative fades in seconds after waking and I cannot remember the exact order of events or what she said. The only lasting impression is fear, a clammy and ugly fear that follows me throughout much of the morning. There is a hunch too that something bad has happened to her or is about to happen to her, because somehow the Kabbalistic word for Satan took shape on her lips.

I wake feeling more anxious than need be, more tired because of that disturbance in the night. I make a mental note to ring Tina. Later when I make it to the office, the first thing I do is to ring the alcohol worker responsible for detox admissions. I argue Tina's case with more conviction, stress how weak she is and how she is sick enough to qualify for a hospital bed independent of any detox considerations. The alcohol worker mentions a long waiting-list and refers to Tina's previous and not very distant detox admissions. But after asking a few more questions the hardness in her voice eases. If she can see Tina a few times at the alcohol groups she runs, she will send the paperwork for detox onto the next stage. It's edging her closer to the detox ward which can save her life. Isn't it important to save a human life? Isn't it something worth working for? Isn't it worth ploughing through yet more paperwork and yet more public sector torpor? Isn't it worth masquerading as a drone for the pharmaceutical industry?

It's a blind spot nobody is very keen to talk about, how so many people are allowed to drink themselves to death. In Tina's case the medical experts understand fully how, if an intervention does not happen very soon, her organs will fail. Resilient as the human body is, it has its limitations. If someone set out to drink household detergent every day it would have a similar effect to the damage the alcoholic causes in the advanced stages of alcoholism. A person habitually drinking detergent is liable to be sectioned under the Mental Health Act and brought to hospital for detoxification and then held against their will for assessment and treatment. But the same citizen causing similar damage to key organs not through drinking detergent but rather from drinking cheap eight or nine percent volume legally bought alcohol would not be sectioned at all. With alcohol the normal rules are put on hold. Alcohol abuse is so prevalent that the current public health regime is limited in when it can use the Mental Health Act for intervention, as there are just too many cases. The will is not there anyway, as alcohol is so easily available and so socially accepted. What would be the point? What would prevent the heavy drinker from just going back out and doing it all over again?

Generally medical professionals are pessimistic on the subject, often accepting that the advanced stages of alcoholism are outside their gift to do much about. They may do all they can under the legislation in place, but they always seem somewhat tired of the whole business. When people are so resolved to drink themselves to death what power on earth can stop them? There is an unspoken acceptance in the medical and psychiatric services of the unusually high percentage of fatalities through alcoholism each year. It is a humiliating, painful death from poisoned blood and failing organs.

For the workers who are the link between the system and the person harmed by acute alcoholism, it is impossible for us not to see those suffering as complex human beings, just as all of us are complex human beings. We do not have the buffer of a clinical or medically professional distance. We are with them in their suffering, sharing in their aspirations for recovery and health. We share too in their frustrations and emotional highs and lows. We do not have the luxury of not believing in secular miracles or even scriptural miracles.

There is a foreboding in the official record of Tina's case as if her GP and the other doctors at the GP surgery and the NHS alcohol workers have already written her off and waved her off to an early and gruelling death, yet another casualty of alcoholism. To be fair there is nothing in her records to suggest otherwise. I ring her and hear in her voice how pleased she is that I have rung. She tells me that she has drunk a glass of milk an hour earlier in a voice sounding like a child trying to please a parent. She talks about her partner and the casual labouring work he has managed to find through his contacts in the local pubs. He is very well known in the area she says. It's obvious he means the world to her. I assure her that I will be over to see her later in the week.

The category of demon, if demon is the right word to use in this context, clinging to the alcoholic in the advanced stages of alcoholism, must be close to McNutt's definition of demons from hell. Equally we can view it as a metaphor. Fetish priests and holistic healers speak of a spirit possession, where the spirit of a departed alcoholic returns to continue Boozing through the conduit of a living entity. It's an idea worth mulling over, especially as our medical diagnostic pathways in tackling alcoholism are far from good when it comes to success rates.

A more conspicuous fact now is that the momentum of complementary, holistic, and spiritual conceptualisations of mental health and addiction healing is propelled by shortcomings and failings in the current models of diagnosis and care. Research tells us that many addictions will run their course over a given span of years. For example, cocaine use will typically last four years. But these are in given cases and cannot be standardised across the entire range of addictions. Medical science reaffirms what we instinctively know, that no one standard fits all.

In the few cases we have looked at so far, the work needed to resolve any of the dilemmas of those in our care is substantial and time-intensive. But I am trapped in an office for an entire morning, caught up in the mindless paper trail of public sector record-keeping, tapping meaningless details onto the coat-tails of a blame culture tinged on all sides by fear. Routine information is duplicated, and the usual mind-numbing bureaucracy is heaped on frontline workers by regulators and managers further up the food-chain, who often appear to have little else to do.

If they were not so obsessed with hog-tying frontline workers with the waste of time their paperwork trail demands, we would be free to work more with our service-users. We would have more freedom to work harder on the most presenting challenges. When travelling to and from appointments, plus paperwork, are pooled together, the equation of face-to-face work to ancillary work can be three to one: one hour actually working with the service-user and three hours staring into a computer screen or sitting on trains and buses. It often feels like there is a mania fixated on the single idea of overloading citizens with as much psychological misery as possible.

Writing in 1933 George Orwell put the obsession with creating unnecessary work down to fear:

> I believe this instinct to perpetuate useless work is, at bottom, simply fear of the mob ... it is safer to keep them too busy to think.

There is hardly a minute's peace from demoralising hype, nudge programming, algorithms, and tacky advertising proclaiming hyper-consumerism and technological fantasies as the highest fulfilment in human freedom and political liberty. In fact a worsening of wages and conditions, addictions, mental illness, physical sickness and disease, employment insecurity, bullying and harassment at work, a range of discriminations, and the mechanisms of stress add up to a crisis serious enough for a major rethink. The idea of progress exists as the drug of choice for those who can't bear for even a moment to accept life as it is. Worship of the future at least takes the mind off the problems of the present.

Any overview is obscured by misinformation. An entire cadre of civil servants have stumbled on a new career direction in manipulating the statistics around unemployment, family breakdown, domestic violence, suicide, alcoholism, NHS malpractice, crime, homelessness, despair in the young, and sexual assault. The list can easily run for several pages. The frontline worker out on the doorsteps of despair might be forgiven for pausing to ask themselves just why they are trying to help save the addicted and the depressed. Is society as it stands worth living in? The masks used in the masquerade can easily slip and fall into the gutter.

To live in the confusion of the crossroads we need a certain knack for living in denial, for understanding at a psychic level how we are existing without important rites and ceremonies linking us to both the living and the dead, while at the same time convincing ourselves it's not so bad. After all, the citizens of lesser countries than ours are said to live worse lives because they are not free. We sacrifice kinship bonds; native spirituality and communion with nature and her cycles; an ancient connection to the land and to our dead; our folklore and customs; our native magic; and our mysticism on the altar of hyper-consumerism and a belief in a secularised idea of progress borrowed from millenarianism and the tawdry projections of morally dubious billionaires and tech gurus strangely detached from the world as it stands. Happy interpretations of technological panoramas of endless hope that are yet to come are used as clubs against our intuition and rationality. If we can only hang on for a bit longer, the future is bound to save us, or so we are told.

In the deficiencies of the macro, we find clues to the spiritual sickness of the individual. If we are to make progress in mental health, it is a prerequisite to hold up to the light of day the idea planted by our psychiatric hierarchy of mental disorder occurring in the brain. Then we are free to search for the origins of the malaise using improved tools of measurement. Instead of healing the psychic and spiritual sickness at the crossroads of our own experience we are obsessed with globalising it, mutating the rest of the world in our image.

What was interesting about the migrant workers I met and worked with in cities like London and Rotterdam was their respect for the business ethic and job-creating genius of advanced countries. But they were dismayed and demoralised at the social, familial, and cultural poverty of these same advanced countries. They would do everything humanly possible to recreate cultural, familial, and spiritual traditions from their own lands in churches, temples, mosques, family units, community centres, and cafés. Rifts between migrant parents and their children who are socialised here were often heartbreaking and sometimes tragic to see unfolding. One ethnic Russian from Lithuania who worked in a Bedfordshire food processing plant summed up the schism of the migrant:

> You have jobs here. Jobs are good. Everything else here is shit!

After hours of dehumanising paperwork, I am freed from the office and finally on the way to see Eddie. I am frustrated after so many hours in front of a computer screen in a stuffy office, tied up in box-ticking exercises to please blame culture managers. Human beings are not designed for prolonged degradation of the spirit, regardless of how the convention of the day insists on the submission of hundreds of millions of people enclosed in the drudgery of open-plan offices. How middle-managers and bosses are not pelted with rotting fruit in the workplace each morning is the crowning achievement of what we know as civilisation.

I meditate as I walk, slowing down my mind and increasing awareness, and I visualise a Theravada master I once studied under. My eyes are open and I am on a busy London street approaching a bus-stop. It's easy to sense the hostility and stress of people waiting at the bus-stop, their unhappiness infectious. I hear an internal chant to Buddha, words of pansil from an orange-robed master sitting in front of the meditation class. A dull gong sounds and there is a scent of sandalwood. Metta, the words of lovingkindness, in the master's soft voice:

> In the beginning-less cycles of existence there is not one sentient being who has not been my friend and relative hundreds of times.

I allow myself the gladness of closing my eyes for a few moments to concentrate on the visualisation of the temple and the meditation class. Simultaneously I am aware of my present reality, aware too of an inner truth inspired by the visualisation of the master at the head of the class:

> One sleeps easily, wakes easily, dreams no evil dreams. One is dear to human beings, dear to non-human beings.

The brief meditation and visualisation reconnect a part of deeper mind to the nurturing instincts in human nature. I am less troubled by the people at the bus-stop who push past in a hurry, less pressured by the tension of their auras. It's not healthy for people to repress so much anger and frustration. It shows in so many gestures and expressions. I take to the top-deck and am lucky to find a seat at the very front. From the windows I look down on London.

In an EEG study in the USA on Metta meditation, volunteers were shown to have alterations in gamma waves and gamma synchronization. Even when not meditating, a brainwave pattern was still present in people practising Metta meditation; it was proven to have changed the workings of the brain. The study also showed a modulation during meditation of the amygdala, the parts of the brain connected to memory, decision-making, and emotional reaction. The study also demonstrated how Metta, or lovingkindness, meditation reduces the participant's tendency to inflammation and distress which are closely linked to major depression, heart disease, and diabetes. The more people meditated using lovingkindness/Metta, the more their brains changed in a way that's beneficial to good health. Meditation was literally boosting their health and raising their consciousness.

The popular therapy for borderline personality disorder known as Dialectical Behaviour Therapy has integrated eastern meditation into its methodology and repackaged it as mindfulness, much as the twelve-step model in the Minnesota Method for addiction recovery borrowed from Judeo-Christian monotheism. The world's spiritual customs can be read as a fount of wisdom and healing, and their messages can be freely heard, as the old book says, by those with ears to hear.

As I think about the positive qualities of Metta, the visualisation of the master at the head of the meditation class fades, leaving only a sweet memory and a sensual residue of sandalwood. The view from the top-deck windows is warmly familiar and I soak up images of a city in motion, as I reconnect with the energy and vitality of London.

I understand more than before that this crossroads has given me far more than I could ever give to it.

As I jump from the bus and set off on foot for the final stretch to where Eddie lives, my phone rings. I now have the opportunity to speak to one of the high priests of our cultural hierarchy. It's a psychiatrist and he wants to talk to me about Eddie. Unfortunately for Eddie the statutory mental health authorities are taking more of an interest in his case. Eddie suffers from what the psychiatrists categorise as obsessive-compulsive disorder and, whether he likes the idea or not, the psychiatrist wants to talk to him about it.

Psychiatrists these days are all touchy-feely and on first name terms with practically everyone, so he insists I call him by his first name, Tristan. He wants to know where I am in my work with Eddie. I am happy to have this rare beast on the other end of the line, this high priest of Western shamanism, this credible juju man with shiny pills bulging in his conjure-bag. I tell him my work with Eddie is mostly practical, involving the finer points of pension-credit, and trying to win him over to the idea of living in a sheltered housing scheme. He has mobility problems and is at the age where he qualifies for a more suitable place to live. With this client, I explain, it's mostly paperwork and lots of patience. It's about smoothing out housing, council tax, and financial details.

Tristan wants to know if Eddie is delusional and I say no more than anyone else I know. Tristan laughs and I laugh too. Tristan is human and wants to be seen as such. He wants to know where and when it would be convenient for him to come and meet me and then for the both of us to visit Eddie. I ask him to hang on and bring up the diary I keep on my phone. I mention an afternoon about a week away and Tristan agrees. I can hear from his voice he is keen to see this man, and I am intrigued to know why he has crossed the radar of this exalted beast of psychopharmacology and social compliance.

In fairness to psychiatrists on the frontline of mental disorder, they need a lot of robustness of character to absorb the projections, grandiosity, arrogance, and pure spitefulness of a percentage of the mentally disordered. Often patients may not have a recognised mental disorder as such, with their problem centring on their personality rather than on a disorder of their thoughts. They can attack at the slightest sign of weakness, pouncing on any expression which could be read as contradictory, dismissive, or vague.

One person diagnosed with schizophrenia, who was supported by our mental health charity, believed companies like Google and Lockheed Martin were controlling people's minds, targeting ordinary people through highly refined technology for their own perverse ends. She badgered and harassed anyone she could, roping the gullible into her delusions, jumping down people's throats the first second she sensed they were questioning her world view. She led people along and then attacked them with passive-aggressive insults: quite a disturbed and disturbing woman.

Any time at all in her company was emotionally draining as her personality was so challenging. Perhaps she was tormented by a heightened awareness of the hellishness of a purely materialist existence. Literalist religions had already hidden so much of the knowledge which would have set her free, so she floundered in ignorance of gnosis and deeper truths known to her ancestors. She was never a minute late for appointments with her psychiatrist. Whatever we think about the motivations of psychiatrists or their kowtowing to the gods of psychopharmacology, they are only human. They are often expected to deal with very difficult personalities and must learn to take personal abuse in their stride. They deal with personalities and psychopaths that most people would run from. They must be professional, or passive in other words, when faced with vile human behaviour and the nastiest of personal insults. For this alone they deserve our respect.

Maybe it's just bad luck. Eddie always comes to me in a sweat of anxiety, burdened by his most recent problem. Usually it's some bureaucratic tangle or other. I advocate for him and reassure him that it will work out okay. It's always a long session where I explain all the finer points of the state's bureaucratic processes and how it all involves him. I explain how I have dealt with letters he has had from official agencies and assure him yet again that he doesn't have to do anything but trust us to advocate for him. He is always impatient, insisting on knowing why certain decisions have not yet been acted on. I remind him that there is a process, just as there is with most things in life. We must wait in the same way that millions of others are waiting.

Government officials or local authority adjudicators are hardly going to drop everything and prioritise a case just because the person in question is impatient. Usually as soon as I finish our work for the day and move on to the next appointment, he hurries to the nearest DWP or council office to hassle them about details they know nothing about.

Once he has got it off his chest he will go about his business. He just needs lots of reassurance from as many sympathetic people as possible in nearly all areas of his life. Somewhere along the line someone must have rang the statutory mental health team to talk about one of his impromptu, frantic visits.

With someone like Eddie any reference, no matter how harmless, to spiritual healing, existential creativity, or holism is a mistake. Any mention of anything not centred on the immediacy of his daily life is a mistake too. Remedies, if there are any remedies, must be hammered out of the practical, tangible facts of his everyday life. All reassurance must be highlighted by common sense and set right in the middle of the starkest reality to hand. All references must be one hundred percent real and as easy as humanly possible to grasp. Anything less will freak him out. He manages his anxiety and impatience through the consolations of a neurotic routine and by exercising as much control as he possibly can over every detail of his life.

Although Cognitive Behavioural Therapy is not as useful as it is claimed to be, it can often help. There are so many fallacies accepted by human consciousness as given truths, so many compelling, credible and emotionally charged falsehoods masked as fact. There is so much confusion and wrong thinking. Somebody must bring it all back to the sober baseline of reality, whether it's a popular thing to do or not. Someone must play the role of Spock in the control room of the Starship Enterprise, reminding an impulsive crew of simple logic. But with the kind of mental health client our charity works with, CBT calls for too much rationality, linguistic communication, and conceptual analysis. By the nature of our work, we are forced way out on the margins of human interaction. The widest lens of holism is needed.

From early on in my first meetings with Eddie I knew all contact had to be practical, as simple as possible, and focused on demonstrable outcomes. Whether I want to or not, I have become a de facto ally in his campaign to control his environment. Through this mostly imagined mechanism of control, I try to lessen the anxiety plucking at the strings of his waking hours. Personal spiritual interests help me to cope with his neurosis and with the consistent force of negative energy he projects onto others. There is no easy way of suggesting to him how a wider, holistic view might help him to manage even some of his anxiety.

It is the norm in most cases for the service users of our mental health charity to be off limits to the possibilities of any kind of rites of personal or higher awareness. They are too oppressed by circumstances, by medication, by the conditioning they've been exposed to all their lives, which prejudice them to new ideas. There is also the problem of weaknesses and underdevelopment of the personality and character. The system wore them down after all, finally convincing them that the problem is primarily a question of chemicals in the brain, and that the remedy is a lifelong obeisance to the gods of psychopharmacology.

Eddie, and the others we support in our work for the mental health charity, are living symbols for all of us, suffering in a time when the absence of moral, community, and spiritual reassurances bring yet more confusion and emptiness into our lives. In this condition we are more malleable in hyper-consumerism's project to transform us into consumers rather than citizens, to break us down into crude buyers of baubles, rather than raising us up into the image of the gods or the god of our hearts. The spiritual, physical, and psychic impositions amount to an attack against reason in itself. If you think I am exaggerating about the degree to which we are brainwashed into conformity, then try this simple experiment.

On the next Saint Valentine's Day, go about your business as normal. Don't bother reserving a restaurant table for two or buying long-stemmed roses or chocolates in a heart-shaped box. Don't buy a Valentine's Day card for your significant other and make no reference to the bombardment of social and media references to Saint Valentine's Day. Try it and see how it goes. If you actually see through such an unthinkable plan, you would understand more fully how the forces of hyper-consumerism are in control of the most intimate parts of our lives.

To defy the orthodoxy of this beast of materialism and psychopharmacological hegemony by referencing the fuller range of human and esoteric factors, is to risk an intimate association with the madness at the heart of the matter. For a frontline support worker employed by a mental health charity to defy the gods of psychopharmacology is to offend the major secular deities, which is an unforgivable insult. I am careful to keep my thoughts to myself. Only when I think a mental health charity service user might really benefit from a disclosure do I disclose. With Big Tam I think it helped in a small way to talk about paganism. The masquerade is real.

If our honest conversation that morning in Kings Cross and hundreds of other disparate experiences, where Tam stretched his conscious thoughts even a little, lead to one moment of self-realisation then holism works. Tam was at the beginning of a journey of experimentation with many further revelations needed to overcome the negativity so damning to his best thinking. We are tangential but important forces in the lives of others because in some cases words and gestures can resonate for an entire lifetime. With an old analogy in mind whereby people influence each other much like the planets influence each other in passing, there is evidence that we influence others more than we think we do.

Likewise with Kenny. We can only hope a ritual to weaken the negative influences of the past helped him in a meaningful way, showing him the fuller reaches of the creative mind. Both Kenny and Big Tam had gravitated beyond the limits of mental health crisis intervention before I met them. They were seen as desperate cases, no-hopers of zero interest to the psychiatric profession. They were unshackled from the mental health system and deemed not only past redemption but ungrateful too. If I had sold them to a murderous gang dealing in human body parts, the psychiatrists who had once managed their care would not have raised an eyebrow. They would probably be equally amazed and impressed that some use was found for them.

Out on those doorsteps of despair we should always be careful not to suggest or initiate esoteric rituals, speak of the arcane, or reference gnosis. Only through the building of trust can rituals and conversations about holism happen. And of course it's about what the client needs and what they are asking for and not about us and our interests. In the circumstances, with causal factors in mind, it is a miracle such conversations and interventions happen at all. The orthodoxy of the day colonises the rational mind, which has been regulated by the state, making it a mind mostly closed to experimental psychology, herbalism, spiritual innovation, and shamanism. The modern mind is often a cerebral version of a puppet on a string. Literalist monotheism ensured the truth of gnosis is not within reach for the masses shepherded into the lower order of power structures, as working drones and birth-givers. Even after so much water under the bridge it continues to be one of their primary roles.

In harmony with the hyper-consumerist ideology of instant gratification, entire populations are seduced into believing in the immediate fix of pharmaceutical drugs. It is not uncommon to hear people insisting on prescriptions for drugs known to have devastating side-effects and very limited positive results. In modern consumerism there's just not enough time. The prescribed pack of pills, whether they work or not, are the best answer to the modern Western condition of perpetual stress and the excessive consumption of time and resources. Just pop a few as you are rushing to your next appointment. If they don't work, then there's always the placebo effect. With Schopenhauer's best thoughts in mind, I am not suggesting there was ever a time in history when consciousness placed lesser pressures on us, but what is stark can under conditions of alienation seem starker.

One problem that comes up repeatedly relating to the current way of doing things is a failure to include holistic and spiritual ideas as part of the general culture of western state psychiatric practice. There is a very simple reason for this: basically they don't want to try. The curative and rehabilitative roles of psychiatry are always secondary to their regulatory role. If society stopped functioning according to the general norms demanded by markets and the aggressive needs of hyper-consumerism, the psychiatric shaman must share in the ensuing blame and gnashing of teeth. Psychiatrists must play their part in the overall game and earn their salaries.

Together with the other branches of medicine, they play a central role in increasing or at least maintaining productivity. Depressed workers must be encouraged to get rid of fanciful and abstract ideas and return to work as quickly as possible, whether the work they do is soul-destroying or not. Mothers struggling to bond with their infants, suicidal pensioners, unemployed young people who have taken to self-harm, as well as skunk-smoking bus-drivers, must be brought back into line so that the bad example of non-conformity does not flare up into a plague of discontent, as it threatened to do during the wilder nights of the Age of Aquarius. Ideas steering the individual too far from the central waters of conformity are to be discouraged at all costs. The normative mechanisms of state psychiatric systems can never be underestimated.

In fairness to the orthodoxy of today, the ideologies of the past are equally unsympathetic towards the cultural and intellectual systems they replaced. The wisdom of ancient cultures, especially Greek, Egyptian, and Roman, was sacrificed to the literalist religious autocracy systematized after Constantine's conversion in AD 324. Constantine's antipathy towards the immense corpus of pre-Christian magic, ritual and tradition, which elevated the ancient world to wondrous heights, set the benchmark for religious intolerance. He purged an empire of knowledge outside a narrow canon of clerical literalism, persecuting

Christian mystics who until his time interpreted Christianity as a restated version of age-old truths.

Humankind adapts to changing conditions and makes the necessary adjustments to survive natural and cultural mutations, as well as the adjustments brought to it by tyrants, and by the tyranny never very far from the human narrative. Yet this doesn't necessarily mean the losses are always tolerable to bear. As far as the primary model of psychiatric assessment is concerned, the initial questions echo trends in popular psychology. Hidden trauma and abuse in childhood are investigated. Dysfunctional family relations and early developmental maladjustment are at the forefront of the interviewer's thoughts. Only the very brave ones mention the reinterpretation of projection as a deflected flaw of personality.

The prevailing view veers towards a critique of the failings of influential figures from the patient's past such as parents, older siblings, or teachers, or towards societal attitudes since deemed to have progressively evolved. Anger and blame are thus redirected. Systems of socialisation, spiritual deficiencies, or the absence of initiation from adolescence into adulthood are excluded. In the interview-type counselling session and assessment process it is always a question of the individual's difficulties in adjusting to the often alienating mutations of radical consumerism and the kind of crass individualism we see everywhere. It is an emphasis in which individuals or traumas from the past might be to blame for maladjustment and how the maladjustments of the past might be corrected. The imbalance of the power dynamic is striking. Questions and assessments are squeezed between the narrowest of margins.

With the structure of assessment as it stands, we will never hear the enlightened interviewer asking the mental health patient sitting in front of them, if they think that the sound chakra in their throat is blocked by mistruth, or that the heart chakra is blocked by a tumultuous loss stretching back to earlier lives. Or perhaps there is a ritual or several interconnected rituals needed to empower the mentally disordered person, so that they can unblock negative emotions from their body and psyche. Or for an experiment in addressing the power dynamic, might we try a session where the patient asks questions of the counsellor or interviewer before the remaining sessions begin?

The questions that honour the potential, fullest integrity, and creative spirit of the human being are never asked. If the rationalist proposes asking them, they would be quickly brought back to the reality of the moment. A tepid deference to a vague political correctness, nothing more than a residue of psychiatric and social care models, sets the standard in the public sector's mental health assessments, pre-detox interviews, and interventions. Normative language and behaviour are the standard by which the work marches forward. The goals are always focused on normalisation and conformity. What truth there is in gnosis and the world of the arcane is not brought up.

Unless an approach of care and healing based on esoteric and holistic principles is organised independently of the state-regulated system, little can be said about outcomes. Cultural prejudice against spiritual freedom of thought is still stubborn. Any mention of the spiritual or the arcane is often wilfully misunderstood as religious doctrine, or as literalist or cultural prejudice. Discourse is doomed to a weary categorisation in the even wearier strictures of what passes as conversation about personal cosmologies and belief systems. What has been classed for centuries as the occult is still potent today, even though many people do not regard it as worth serious investigation. The work of wiping out our ancient wisdom, started so enthusiastically by Constantine and by so many exoteric religious fanatics, is continued today by hyper-consumerism.

We are all involved in an ongoing experiment at this crossroads. Mental health assessments are not addressed to the macro, or to matters related to the dead who went before us. Like any orthodoxy, ours dislikes dissent and is quick to react to it. As charity-sector mental health workers, we deal with its unwilling dissenters every day, often sensitive souls who have deteriorated in their thinking in a time and place stripped of cosmological and spiritual meaning, kinship bonds, mystery, and a meaningful community. Others either internalise the darkness and confusion of the crossroads or attract the spiritual entities known throughout the ages as "demons". They understand at a psychic level that we were created by an eternally ignorant demiurge but that there is a spark of divinity inside us, a divinity connected to an unknowable god. But all knowledge of these facts is denied to them by so many humanised serpents who worship materialism and the demon-gods of materialism. Through the centuries these have pointed to scriptures much like the slave master pointed to the cart whip. To work under such serpents in human form, we must pull off a convincing masquerade.

Eddie is not pleased to see me. At least he doesn't show any of the recognisable signs of welcome. On a previous visit he shouted at me the second I stepped into his room. Perhaps it was more like a scream, or somewhere between a scream and a shout. His voice then broke at the peak of his "shouting scream" and he glared at me in a rage from across the room. My crime was to take a step in the direction of a chair he didn't want me to sit in. It wasn't that I had tried to upset him by sitting somewhere he didn't want me to sit. I innocently took a step towards the nearest chair not knowing Eddie wanted me to sit in a chair in another corner of his room. To be fair I didn't read it as so unreasonable; after all we were in his home, a single room in a shared house of often insensitive strangers. Doesn't everyone want to control at least one part of their life? And controlling who sits where in a cramped rented room doesn't seem so obsessive in a time of obsession.

Outside, in the world as we know it, things are different. The greengrocer at the end of the street banned Eddie from his shop for messing about with fruit. He stood for ages weighing an apple in each hand as he couldn't decide which one to buy. Minutes passed and there he stood, agonising over which piece of fruit to pick. Apparently it was a regular performance, and the greengrocer finally lost patience and banned him from his shop. It adds up to a lot of stress, deliberating like that in public over a piece of fruit.

It seems like Eddie had a taste of what the psychiatric services were like back in the nineteen eighties or thereabouts. Whatever happened back then, he has shown real canniness to avoid a repeat of it. Most of his belongings are packed in several antiquated suitcases and stacked against one wall. The others who live in the house are strangers who often stampede up and down the stairs past his room with little or no thought for the peace of others. He has a private pension and savings, so he does not have to live like this. Several social care professionals have tried to talk him into signing up for a flat in a sheltered scheme.

But for vague reasons, which change regularly, he refuses. He knows his alleged madness would be far more obvious in the observed corridors and communal spaces of a sheltered housing scheme. In the house of squalor he lives in, the standards of mental health and general behaviour are not high. In such places people keep their wackiness and selfishness to themselves. It would take quite a scene or performance to distract the people living in the other rooms from the dramas of their lives. But Eddie's getting to an age where climbing in and out of a bathtub without specially fitted grips is impractical. His knees are succumbing to the years and for simple expediency he needs to live somewhere on a ground-floor.

Now that I have sat where he wants me to sit, we can begin the work in hand. It's all routine, letters to government departments, a council tax readjustment, a passport renewal application. Eddie is petulant every step of the way. He is obstructive and very slow to disclose the information needed for the paper trail. He shouts out at times because of what he sees as corruption and incompetence in the systems we must deal with.

I know that he would redirect the rage of blame my way in a second. The various advice centres, charities, and non-governmental support services in this part of London know him well. If a worker reminds him of actual reality or asks a question even remotely personal, he will ask to be transferred to another worker. Or he will disengage straight away from their service or agency. He is on a full-time flight from his own psychic reality, free running from the stress of his inner life. He is on the run from the statutory mental health services too, but his luck is fast fading.

The more I get to know him the more I like and respect him, even though he can be a difficult, complex man. He has hinted often enough at psychological demons chasing him through the decades, but any time I have tried to tease these hints into a conversation he has changed the subject. He is a trim, very neat man in his mid-seventies who would never dream of leaving his room without an immaculate shirt and tie. Slacks and sports-jacket fit like a second skin. He spit-polishes his shoes barrack-room style, then buffs them with a chamois.

He has worked as a skilled technician for most of his life. After he retired, he worked part-time in unskilled jobs. He is a decent, moral, compassionate man with fundamental Christian convictions. On the couple of occasions when he has mentioned the Christian messiah, his proud grey eyes misted a little and his lips quivered. He has a few close friends, mostly women, and goes to a church service most Sundays. He keeps his homosexuality tightly under wraps. His worst fears and anxieties seem to vacillate between his suppressed sexuality and the thought of once more crossing the radar of the state's mental health authorities. He is from a generation where homosexuality was so taboo it would not be surprising if he was held against his will in one of the old mental hospitals largely because of his sexual orientation. Homosexuality is more understandable as a taboo, when birth-rates were critical for the survival of city states, nations, and tribes. When such necessity had lessened, the prejudice lingered and was made stronger by literalism's unimaginative blueprint, and the cruelty never far removed from the human condition. Sodom and Gomorrah were wrongly held up as warnings against homosexuality but are in fact part of a morality tale where a threatened sexual assault against the emissaries of God was punished by the divine will. It is harder now in an age of population growth and secularism to expect people to believe that tribal rituals and religious prejudice from an era long passed into ancient history are meaningful in their lives.

The literalist word from monotheistic religions was finally exposed as an instrument of power used by hierarchies. The true spiritual path has always been about inner transformation. The expansion of consciousness has little to do with blindly following literal translations from the aspirations of nomads surviving in a hostile world, although to survive in the world a number of faces must be worn at various times. When gay people are demonised by religious followers using age-old denunciations, their denouncers are as much a victim of the disgust at the human condition at the heart of scriptural literalism as their victims.

What happened to Eddie? Did he internalise parental literalism so that he became his own worst critic, condemning his own nature with cruel judgements from the desert nomads of the Old Testament? The same nomads cast out their kin to die and stoned their own children to death for transgressions now laughable and incomprehensible. How religious literalism still holds such a grip on the minds of so many today is one of the modern world's conundrums. Its influence can never be underestimated. The rationalist must guard against dangerous seeds literalist irrationality plants in the conscious mind, and in the regions of mind beyond the conscious. Many general truths to do with our human encompassment are an achievement of the scriptures, but there are ciphers and hidden truths too, mysteries and baffling asides that the modernist rarely has time for in a more time-harried age.

If a mistruth is repeated often enough, it takes its place in the culture as fact. The prejudices of religious literalism mutate truth into mistruth over generations. Eddie, sadly, is one of literalism's victims, crushed as he is by a mind contaminated in its earlier years by literalist narrowmindedness. He was brought up in a small coastal town by Salvationists, but he doesn't want to say much more on the matter.

As the old folk saying goes, "every cripple has his own way of walking". Eddie has adapted and walked through the decades with his neckties always perfectly knotted and his loyalty to literalist monotheism intact.

The principles and possibilities of reincarnation are absent in our psychological models of personal identity. In an overall view of global spiritual traditions, reincarnation is familiar. If we have been reborn many times, then there is a likelihood that we have experienced a past life in the gender opposite to the one we currently live with. Man lived as woman, woman as man. The heavy shroud of religious literalism, often used to bring people together in much harder times, obscures objective views of this transgender chain of life. Repetition through generations of redundant tales of the doomed inhabitants of Sodom and Gomorrah brings up yet more misunderstanding and intolerance of otherness. As recently as the 1830s men in England were executed for the crime of sodomy. The laws were only relaxed in 1967 to allow sexual intercourse between men, with the caveat of there being no third person present. The misery, blackmail, suicidal ideation and actual suicide, humiliation, and psychological pressure this caused to so many people weigh against our culture's earlier claims of moral authority and enlightenment.

The Navajos of North America recognise four rather than two distinct genders: Dilbaa (masculine woman); Nadleehi (feminine man); Hastiin (masculine man); and Asdzan (feminine woman). Dilbaa and Nadleehi are seen to be two-spirited people, and as such are honoured and regarded as spiritually gifted. In the west the homosexual taboo was dragged through the centuries like a bloodied fetish. In real terms there are only two genders but in the nuances of a fallen world there ought to be time and space to look deeper into the psychic origins of identity. In hindsight it is easier to understand the psychiatric outpatient burdened by literalist fanaticism as another interpretation of the trickster from the folklore of the Winnebagos in North America, whose penis is carried in a box and head trapped in an elk's skull.

Sexuality comes to mind because I can imagine that it's had quite a bearing on Eddie's personal development and inner life. During Eddie's formative years, his blossoming sexuality was illegal. What way out did he have from such a taboo? He had to go through it, and he carries it in the stress of his obsessive-compulsive disorder. It cannot be stated as an absolute truth, that Eddie or anyone else might be influenced in their sexuality because of a spiritual or psychic link to a previous life lived in the opposite gender. But at moments of confusion or doubt it might help to remember such a possibility.

We have managed to get through the paperwork we needed to get through. He hasn't shouted yet or banged a fist hard on the table. It's easier now to sense the pressure he places himself under, the pressure he has carried through the decades. He collects guilt too, mostly from television and radio shows, from fragments of conversations overheard at laundrettes. And from the supermarket queues and at the transport cafés he visits daily. He's a living magnet for stress. If a politician is spouting the expected line with cheap publicity in mind, he takes it personally. He often feels guilty about it. Once he heard a female politician on television making a broad point about how men ought to take more responsibility for their children. He felt guilty about it for days after, even though he doesn't have children and is unlikely at this stage in his life to acquire any.

His guilt and sexual oppression are dwarfed by his hatred of the state psychiatric system. I know he has had at least one admission in the past. Where exactly it happened and what exactly the circumstances were, he's not saying. There is a dark hint now and then, a pause and a look stating all he really needs to state. He tolerates me because I work for a charity and focus on the practical social care work keeping the whole neurotic show on the road. I know that if I mention Tristan the friendly psychiatrist there will be uproar, probably a major one. In fact, if I make any reference at all to mental health or even by accident use the word mental in a sentence, there will be trouble. When not fixated on his own contrariness, he is a humane and humorous man. When he talks about the people he meets in the course of an ordinary day and the incidental conversations he finds himself caught up in it is impossible not to laugh. At times we laughed together. He doesn't realise how naturally funny he is or what a charming man lies beneath all the stress.

I walk a short distance on life's road with Eddie. In the circumstances it's all the role requires. I cannot protect him against Tristan because Tristan is a high priest of the mental health orthodoxy. I am nothing but a version of the concerned neighbour walking a stretch of the road with a troubled man, an esotericist masquerading as an outrider for psychopharmacology. Somewhere along the way Eddie stepped over the line in his conversations with the people or the agencies he regularly speaks with. Now Tristan the psychiatrist from the older persons' team is homing in on him. I just hope I am not around on the glum day they finally meet, but I sense I won't get off the hook so easily. I know Tristan will need someone to arrange a meeting between him and the man he is so keen to meet. And I will be seen as just another pawn closing off Eddie's escape route on the chessboard.

The old asylums were closed down for the most part by the 1990s, so he might easily have been admitted to one of them during a trauma of one kind or other, voluntarily or involuntarily. West Park, Friern Barnet, Hanwell, Cane Hill. Others too, ringing London like watchtowers of regulation in a pre-globalised society. In appearance they were not unlike a visualisation of Mervyn Peake's Castle Gormenghast. Lonely laneways meandered through blissful but always slightly sinister countryside to arrive unexpectedly at grandly austere mid-Victorian facades. The old Cane Hill Asylum crops up in the footnotes of popular culture because relatives of famous Londoners were held there for years or even decades, or they committed suicide there.

Around the time I was working with Eddie, I went to the site of the old Cane Hill Asylum to look around at what was left to see. It's easy enough to get there via a train connection from East Croydon to South Coulsdon. The walk from the station to the asylum is uplifting to urbanites at a distance from nature. Placid, friendly old ponies graze on the hill's incline. The surrounding hedgerows and ancient old chestnut trees are alive with birdsong. Halfway up the hill I look back to see roads clogged with frantic volumes of traffic, and cranes rising high in the air like metallic monsters on ominous, misanthropic duties. Modernity is nudging its way unapologetically into these green fields, with the days of birdsong and greenery numbered. The shadows of construction cranes are already zig-zagging its slopes.

It doesn't take much imagination to create a mental picture of what it was like to get off the train at South Coulsdon and walk to the Cane Hill Asylum a few decades earlier, when the wards were filled to capacity. About halfway up the hill on the road winding towards what remains of the asylum, two dogwalkers run from behind foliage on an embankment high on one side of the road. Their dogs run giddily ahead of them. They are energetic women in tracksuits, fleeced jackets, and suburban bobs. It seems that they know the land and are taking a shortcut through a copse of embankment saplings. The dogs are friendly. One of them scampers close to me and yelps. The owner calls out to say the dog is harmless, and I compliment her on keeping such a happy animal.

I ask them if I am near the site of the old asylum. They point up ahead and say it's barely ten minutes that way. They warn me about the security at the Cane Hill site, and that they and other dogwalkers have been stopped and hassled on various parts of the hill. I ask if this is not a public road, and they say yes, it is. But still the security patrols prowl the hill in land rovers, bothering people who are walking their dogs or taking shortcuts they have taken all their lives. Apparently the heavy-handed security is justified because urban explorers, vandals, and curious locals have trespassed on the site in the past.

I thank the dog-walkers and continue in the direction they've pointed me in. I am half-expecting a Land Rover from the Cane Hill security team to screech around the bend in the road at any second. Even with vandals and urban explorers in mind, it is still odd to see so much security on what is just a construction site. What exactly are they guarding? A little further on I pass rusted old road-signs pointing to the hospital and further on there are security gates to stop vehicles taking the narrow slip road leading to the Cane Hill site. At this exact point I feel strangely alone. The sensation is not just because I am physically alone, as it is obvious I am on a hill close to what remains of one of the old London asylums, and there is nobody else in sight. It is a more niggling kind of loneliness. It's a kind of loneliness it would not be good to get used to having.

I trudge on up the hill with trees and serene green fields all around me. What should be an inspiring walk in the countryside isn't inspiring at all. I feel anxious, isolated and conscious of an odd mood of sadness. When I make it to the security fence, I can see what remains of Cane Hill: the water-tower, administration block, and chapel. Everything else has fallen to the demolition bulldozers. I loiter by the chicken-wire fence taking in what is left of the old asylum and then follow the fence for about two hundred yards. At this point I am as close as I am going to get to the chapel. The signs warning off trespassers are very clear. A guard-dog barks from a distant part of the site.

I have visited haunted locations since childhood, and once spent a long day at Auschwitz, both in the museums and in the surrounding forests and villages. I have been to Dachau and to sites in the Ardennes where prisoners of war were shot out of hand. I have explored houses where terrible crimes happened, and in a few of those places sensed the extramundane in both mind and body. The site of the old Cane Hill Asylum is far more disturbing than any of the ominous places I have visited before. A troubled aura infests the entire location. I remain here both fascinated and repelled by the pulsations of negative energy. The human sufferings through time are conspicuous. People have passed on without due respect and ritual. Their etheric and astral bodies are still drawn to this earthly location where they had suffered most. In other words, the place is haunted.

People lived and died here with unusual sadness in their hearts and without a moment's true peace or consolation. Their mental disorders were not properly responded to by society, by their peers, or by their friends and families. In most cases it wasn't mental illness but rather a spiritual malaise, demon possession, or serious family, emotional, or social problems. With the routes to knowledge of the arcane long sealed or obliterated by new gods of materialism and ego, where can the sensitive soul even begin the journey to self-knowledge? Some of the departed souls have not gone far from Cane Hill. They are still drawn to the scene of suffering as earthbound spirits. I can sense these impressions as unambiguously as the autumn sun on my face and the breezes against my skin. When I turn to walk away from the security fence ringing the site, the sadness intensifies. Do the departed inmates of the old asylum need our prayers?

As I walk down the hill towards South Coulsdon station, the sadness and sense of tragedy lighten with every step. I notice again how beautifully the birds in the hedgerows are singing, and I appreciate the serenity of the hillside. It feels as if I am walking away from a scene of terrible sadness and regret. It's understandable why the souls who are not here in this realm of the senses are so desperate to leave the scene too, if only they had the means to leave.

At South Coulsdon station I am happy to be around people again. For the remainder of the day, I am torn between two very different emotions. On one hand, there's a joy to be physically free from Cane Hill and its surroundings. On the other, there is sadness darkened with vague impressions of guilt as I walk away from what was once a human sanctuary and is now so in need of solace. I carry a chunk of sadness with me on the journey home. It's hard not to notice how people on the train are looking at me strangely. The unusual looks and unkind glances are somehow linked to my visit to the site of the old Cane Hill asylum.

The people on the train feel the chill of their own death in the aura I have unwillingly carried with me from the troubled spirituality of the old asylum. And they duly look at me with ice-cold eyes. They cannot understand what they are sensing in my presence, but they know it is anything but joyful or comforting. If ever a site is begging for the sanctifying rites of an interdenominational service, it's the ground and buildings remaining from the old Cane Hill Asylum.

I have to go. Eddie wants to talk more about the council tax letters he has just had in the post, but I have already explained their meaning, and how I sorted them out on an earlier visit. Maybe he's lonely and wants to talk some more for the simple satisfaction of communicating with another human being. I remember reading about a loneliness epidemic in developed countries, and how in Japan pensioners who have led exemplary lives are now committing petty crimes in the hope of getting sent to jail, as anything is better than the loneliness of their ordinary lives. That's extreme but it makes sense. Are we next in line for that?

I cannot help wondering if he spent time at Cane Hill or a similar institution. Emotionally it is possible to connect the aversion he has to any type of psychiatric intervention with the sorrow and dread yet haunting Cane Hill. There is a real link there between Eddie and the tragedy of the old asylums. Who knows what he went through? It's not inconceivable that they treated him for his sexual impulses. Or maybe he was traumatised by spiritual invasion from the suffering of others or from the ghosts of former patients. Whatever it was, it left him in terror of the psychiatric services. And a walking, talking variant of this terror is waiting around the corner in the guise of Tristan the local mental health trust's friendly psychiatrist.

On my way out he is shouting a string of instructions, pleadings, and complaints. Then his tone defaults to an irritating whine people find difficult to listen to for longer than a few minutes. He is asking the questions he's asked for much of the hour and a half we have sat together in his room. At this frantic crossroads he is expected to handle it all, the anxieties of the average consumer in an age of isolation, the extremes of loneliness in a lonely age.

He is not cut out for it. And probably at the root of all this obsessive compulsiveness is the fact that he's not cut out for this way of living. By temperament and psychology, he is more suited to the structure and reassurances of communal life, of a tribal or Polynesian existence touched by nature, sunshine, and the reassurance of immutable social laws and familial relationships. Maybe most of us long for such conditions, or at least subconsciously long for a hunter-gatherer life far away from flashing neon signage and the eternal light from computer screens;

also from the hatred of advertisers with a malice behind their slice-of-life drivel as bad as most demonic attacks. But we're still here, along with Eddie. We are here on the cusp of a strange new world prodded on all sides by technological innovation, with implications we can only pretend to understand.

He is calling out in a louder voice as I hurry down the stairway of the house of multiple occupation. I call back over one shoulder to reassure him that there's nothing to worry about, his paperwork is in order. There's a part of me conditioned by the general shape of life most of us know into seeing him as needy, neurotic, and pedantic. But, pausing to see past an outer veneer formed of stress, there is just an ordinary man caught up in an endless silent scream of protest and outrage, a man without much in the way of guidance from enlightened elders or knowledge of the arcane. Whatever was intended to nurture him has almost destroyed him. He finds himself dependent on state agencies, cold and baffling in their bureaucracy, and confusing in their communications. And always there's a terror hanging over his head that one day what happened to him in a state psychiatric faculty will happen all over again.

Out in the street I check my phone and find missed calls and text messages from the more desperate cases we're supporting in the community or whatever constitutes a community in this part of town. They have addictions and avoid the fuller reality of their own consciousness by wiping out their powers of reason with tins of cheap gut-rot alcohol, and the chemically altered strain of cannabis known as skunk, or sucking on laughing-gas balloons, or drawing into their lungs and bloodstream the highly toxic and addictive poison we know as the modern cigarette. Later when the synthetic cannabis known as spice is sold along with sweets and newspapers in corner shops they will use that too. When the authorities finally wake up and ban spice, the same people will buy it illegally from street-dealers at several times its cost. They cement their own destruction with whatever else street-corner drug peddlers are touting at present. It's slow and painful suicide. Occasionally they call my number to shout out raging demands for instant answers.

The NHS drug and alcohol teams and psychiatrists haven't got the answers either. If the addicted man or woman is fortunate enough to stay alive through a tempest of addiction, they might hear the answer they're looking for in the forum of their own deeper thoughts.

Already too many of them are dying or going past a point of no return. In any analysis of the defining highs and lows in the development of their addictions, it is difficult not to identify most of the disaster as a series of extremely bad decisions at key moments when bad decisions were not the requirement. Causal factors behind these decisions are the key to the truth of addiction. The truth is within but there is no money or status to be won by telling others that the answers they are seeking in their deepest dreams can be found there. It's not our role to cure alcoholism and drug addiction, even though this is often implied by the harassed social workers and social care managers further up the food chain. The tide is turning against us. Too many vulnerable adults with chronic and severe alcoholism and drug addiction are falling to an agonising and humiliating death. In the spirit of holistic healing and the arcane surely there is more we can do or at least try to do.

The evening before I had read a little from the *Dhammapada* and a few pages from other eastern texts, trying to reconcile theories of awakened consciousness with my experience of psychiatric care. Elevation and intensification of consciousness are absent in psychiatry and psychoanalysis, insofar as our practitioners don't appear to be aware of eastern theories of consciousness. What is the nature of our consciousness? Are we really fast asleep even in our most lucid moments, not even remembering ourselves when in a reflective mood? I wonder if this is really what psychiatric patients are trying to do, to wake up from a condition of deep psychic sleep. Or are they troubled because their consciousness can grasp the necessity of waking from such a profound psychic sleep, to finally begin the journey towards gnosis? And, if this is the case, is it the psychiatrist's job to put them back to sleep again?

There is a need for a more potent philosophy, more insight, wisdom and direction freed from the complacent, self-serving, and confusing system we are caught up in. I am compelled to open a door into the mysteries that is more often avoided than embraced, to take to the *Ginza* and *The Great Song to Mani* like a Manichaean poet. Getting into a little mysticism with a focused mind after all tempts interesting outcomes. And so again my thoughts turn in this direction but rather than visiting the experiments of the past, there are braver directions to find.

The mind of the 19th century French Kabbalist and master of the esoteric Éliphas Lévi was in conflict with the more unimaginative forces of religious convention and autocracy. Through his inspirational books and esoteric pamphlets, Lévi tried to reconcile the spiritual principles and practices of the west with the teachings of the Roman church he was born into and where he served as a seminarian and deacon. Western churches had plenty of scope to mature their dogma at key moments in the history of Christianity. History records how so many opportunities to do so were doomed through fear of heresy, hierarchical protectionism, love of power and money, and a ruthless partnership when needed with temporal powers.

Why Lévi believed he might influence such a settlement is a fascinating question in itself. Much of what Christian esotericists like Lévi were advocating can be found in the earlier practices of the Church before Constantine. But the imagination and humility required on behalf of monotheistic hierarchies to acknowledge at last their maverick offspring was as absent in Lévi's time as much as it is now. The decline of western spirituality is morbidly linked to the rationalist expansion of the Western mind. It is also linked to the failure to listen to the silenced voices of the past. Little has changed since Lévi's day except that churches are emptier, and the level of debate is less to the point. The true hope for the old western churches is to embrace their own esoteric past, to accept the experimentation of the congregation's wilder spirits. Otherwise they risk being haunted by the ghosts of their most talented progeny and laughed at by so many of the humanists and secularists that they have created.

In a quest for truth and for a revised view on the dilemmas and destinies of the mentally disordered men, the search goes on for answers outside the literalist citadels of wisdom. We reach for the esoteric when we know from our own tainted experience and from the lessons of history that the deeper truths of individual journeys are not on offer from monotheistic religions in their present set-up. Nor can we find them in the inflexibility of literalism. However, there are still possible answers and other routes forward.

It is inspiring to touch wisdom and healing not easily reached by an internet search or through whispered conversations in the corridors after the Maudsley Debates. It is a fount of illumination open to all who are ready to push fear and narrow-mindedness to one side. It is an odyssey to our collective unconscious and to the fringes of the Astral Plane, an expedition to the base of our mental lives at the very gates of eternity itself, to the gnosis at the cusp of our being.

Solomon

Tina is dead. I take the call late in the shift. Someone from the NHS who also had input into her care rings me. It is nice of him to take the time to call, as people often don't bother in this line of work. He does not know much other than she had taken ill at home and her partner called an ambulance. She died on the way to hospital, from organ failure apparently. I thank him again. After we finish speaking, I try to ring her partner but can't get through.

Tina was a charming, quirky, interesting person and we couldn't save her. Whatever the NHS, social services, and our mental health charity were doing, it didn't work. We didn't do enough. We didn't try enough angles or methods. We were on the way to getting her out of the slum where she lived. She was close to another detox admission. But, all in all, the collective efforts to save her were puny. For Tina the permissive society was too permissive. Surely nobody should be allowed to simply drink themselves to death. There are times where it is possible to hear the rudest laughter of an ignorant creator, and in the hours after her death such laughter could be faintly heard.

I am careful as I go about the routines of the day; phone-calls to the various agencies we liaise with, and official records of the work we do on behalf of our addicted and mentally disordered vulnerable adults.

There is a dull, impassive meridian to uphold, a middle-ground not too critical of the mental health charity's outpatients. Equally we must not be seen to be on their side. I have been suspended in the past for caring too much for the mental health outpatients and vulnerable adults I had been employed to care for, even though the care I was giving at the time was not in any way over the top.

Once I was working through an agency as a mental health project worker in a hostel on a quiet residential street just off Highgate Hill, only a five-minute walk from Highgate Village. On one evening shift I was the only worker on duty when a community psychiatric nurse brought in a patient to begin his post-discharge rehabilitation. It was the day staff's responsibility to prepare the room the new patient was moving into, and they had done nothing. They hadn't even bothered mentioning that a new patient was on his way before they went off shift. There was no lightbulb and no bedclothes in the room. The sink and floor were filthy. I apologised to the community nurse and to the patient. Then I set to work and cleaned the sink and floor and scavenged a lightbulb from another part of the building. I remembered coming across an old duvet and pillow stuffed into a binbag at the bottom of a cupboard in the office a little earlier. I dug out the duvet and pillow and offered them as a makeshift plan for the coming night.

The mental health patient who had come straight from an acute ward could not have been more understanding and accepted that it was a mistake. I promised it would be sorted out the next day. When the manager showed up in the morning, she was disgusted that I had taken any trouble at all to help the new arrival. Within minutes she rang the agency to cancel any further shifts I was pencilled in for. She told the agency she did not want me there as I had misused bed coverings. So much of the humanist project of progress is an illusion, often no more than a veil over a gaping wound not many want to look at for long.

Another manager hounded frontline workers for what he saw as our consistent kindness to mental health patients. He went out of his way to humiliate us in front of colleagues after noticing that a few of us were slow to join in the normalised regime of humiliation. He saw that we preferred a more holistic or humane outlook and took it personally and pressurised us until there was no choice but to leave. I suppressed all feelings on the matter and made an excuse that something personal had come up. There was no recourse to a fair hearing as the managers and HR department simply close ranks when complaints are made.

There was no effective unionisation, as is often the case in entire sectors of the UK's workforce. You suck it up or move on. Nobody cares what option you take. Often nobody cares full stop.

The situation became far worse than it was to begin with. The only sane thing to do was to hide what I truly felt about this manager and his passive-aggressive bullying, and find a way out of there. The alternative was several months of stress, loss of earnings, and time-wasting at the employment tribunal, and no sane person has time for that. But the harassment left a mark on me, and I couldn't just shrug it off. I tried to, but my feelings were too raw. I knew I would have to find a more personalised way of dealing with the fuller inferences of what happened.

I discussed it with a friend, a former Orthodox monk who had spent over a decade in prayer and isolation high in the Ethiopian mountains. He made a wax effigy of the manager and gathered graveyard dirt, a phial of blood, and black candles for a spell. I knew it had the potential to call down violent entities from the Astral Plane. The words alone are chilling. When the ritual is followed through to the last detail, it counts as a malignant piece of magic. He translated it from Ge'ez and warned me never to use it lightly. On the night he suggested we use the spell, I had second thoughts. We had cut out a photo of the manager from a mental health newsletter and placed it close to the effigy and the other accoutrements of magic. I had a strong sense that if I went ahead with the curse it would be fatal.

To focus the human will through the ritualised curse while troubled with negative intensity could have killed the subject, or at least harmed him permanently. All in all, it was a dark time. I had greatly suffered from the manager's hatred, as we were just working together in the same environment and had no contact or shared interests outside work. Energy flowed from his psyche as a single-minded protest at my very presence or what my presence symbolised at the source of his projections. I wondered if I too might die, if we worked out an unholy damnation refined through the centuries in the mountain caves of Ethiopian Orthodox monks. Was there any real way of knowing what could happen if we conjured such a hex with such forceful personal energy involved?

There was a real chance of something happening, something beyond the control of mere men, such was the power of the ancient hexing ritual and the extremes of emotions involved. There was a significant possibility of a fatality. I didn't want the death of a man on my hands, for such a death would have to be accounted for further on up the road. So, I gathered up the magical paraphernalia, chucked it in the bin, thanked my Ethiopian friend, and said it would be best to just forget about the whole business. It was the wisest thing to do. But even the momentary proximity of the manager's photograph and effigy to the Ge'ez symbols etched in blood had a bad outcome.

A day or two later I learnt that the manager we had intended to hex was seriously sick at work with a gastric bug. Someone had to drive him to the nearest casualty department, and he had left a trail of bodily effluence from more than one orifice in the hallway of the mental health hostel. I learnt a lot from the experience. I am sure if I had gone ahead with the hexing spell, he would not have survived. I don't even know if I would have survived it either. For a few nights afterwards I sensed the presence of entities from the Astral Plane, strange mutations of energies flitting here and there and then quickly dissipating. They did more than hint at a willingness to react to the ancient Ge'ez invocation.

I know it sounds pathetic but many of the managers of London's mental health charity hostels and services are simply unsuited to positions involving human beings, vulnerable or otherwise. They are often unknowingly sadistic, acting out on ugly traits of character: Perls's "unadmitted cruelties" of the personality. Others have a sharp critical parent in the workings of their minds, as understood in the logic of Transactional Analysis. Or they are slyly abusive to the disempowered in their care. They often employ cronies or disposable agency staff and are expert bullies and harassers. Temporary workers are sent back to their agencies on spurious grounds, if the energies they give to the care of the clients threaten the manager's conceit or warped sense of what the job entails.

It happened several times when I was caring as competently as I humanly could. But in caring in a compassionate way I failed to mirror the systemic indifference, calculated cruelties, corporate values, or psychopharmacological ethos of the systems in place. So I am always careful not to give the impression that I really care, and not to go beyond the norm to try and help work through the dilemmas in the lives of these vulnerable adults. I genuinely care for Tina, Kenny, Nicos, and the others, but don't wear my heart on my sleeve when recording work with them in notes and risk assessments. I have been sent back to agencies too many times or been misunderstood wilfully or otherwise by managers. I am restrained in how I record Tina's death as we cannot afford anyone in authority to think we care too much.

Her death hangs over the day as I catch a bus to where Solomon lives. Death and the wider connotations of death are everywhere on my journey to see this gentle fellow. The year before, I had worked with a psychiatric nurse who had dropped dead in his forties, even though he was a fit man with no apparent underlying health problems. Everyone was saddened by the news. It just didn't make sense. There was no clear explanation as to what had caused his death.

People who knew him mentioned stress as a causal factor as he worked exceptionally hard. I hadn't heard anyone linking his sudden death with his management of several seriously mentally disordered patients living in shared flats. In earlier years the patients in question would never have been released to live independently because of the severity of their mental conditions and the risks to themselves that independent life would involve. They were not criminally violent as such or antisocial, but very disturbed. One of them was almost certainly in the category of what authorities on evil spirits describe as possessed by "demons from hell".

I sensed that the nurse in question exposed himself needlessly to waves of all the wrong kind of energy from his patients. I mentioned this to him once. When I asked if he did anything to protect himself spiritually from the consequences of his work, he laughed the question off. He looked at me as if he doubted my mental balance or was waiting for a joke to come. He said he was a non-believer and did not bother with unscientific ramblings and superstition, and he changed the subject in seconds. Not long afterwards he was dead. Yet again someone mistook psychic awareness for submission to the often poorly communicated creeds of literalist monotheism, and in doing so missed the point.

My reflections on death continue as far as Solomon's front door. I pause for a minute or two before I press the doorbell to try and purge my thoughts of traces of death. I deflect memories from the last conversation I shared with Tina and concentrate on the flaming sword from the banishing ritual, and I close my eyes to picture it circling overhead protectively. At the same time, I draw a pentagram in the air with the middle and index fingers of my right hand and murmur words of power. I run rosary beads through my fingers. There's not much time to renew mental energy on this morning. Anyhow, I am standing in public view on the balcony of a council housing block. I am not in the right mental space to be of much help to complex needs adults, not with death everywhere in my thoughts. But mercifully it's Solomon I am here to see.

When I ring the doorbell he is slow to answer. I can hear him moving about inside so I know he is in there. He is as polite as ever and invites me in with the gentle deference that is never too far from his words or gestures. The interior of his flat is dark and cheerless with nothing by way of ornament, personal effects, or mementoes to suggest that anyone lives here. On an earlier visit the kitchen was so filthy I insisted that we both rolled up our sleeves and sorted it out.

Today it's better. There are no health and safety outrages to sidetrack us. We sit in the kitchen as it's the only room with chairs: two hard, wooden chairs I scrounged several weeks before from a charity with a furniture store. As ever, Solomon tilts forward with his elbows on his knees and his face is placid, as close to expressionless as the human face ever can be. On an earlier visit he assured me he no longer goes for days and nights without sleep, and eats every day or at least every other day.

Part of our role is to guide outpatients like Solomon towards meaningful activities, to motivate them to volunteer for a good cause or enrol on a college course. Or I must find a way of inspiring him to take part in even a small way in the world most of us inhabit. But he is not interested. He gives the impression that anything outside his own thought-life is immaterial. On a good day he might talk about whatever I suggest for a few minutes out of politeness, but he will promptly drift off again.

It then becomes more noticeable that he is actually tuned into the energy of another sun. He is complying with the meds they have given him for depression. But it's questionable whether they have any real effect on his overall outlook and daily life. I have worked with him when he was unmedicated, lightly medicated, and when he was prescribed different meds. Through each stage he was the same man. The fluctuations in medication give us something to talk about as there are physical side-effects to do with appetite, sleeping-patterns, energy levels, and so on. But the underlying question of his depression is unchanged.

Eventually I get it and understand his impasse. I know spiritually he is grounded and succoured by an ancient faith. There's no impression of a disconnection with his ancestors or of any underlying psychic malaise. He has retreated into the sphere of his brain where he is most at ease, spending hour after hour lost in his own thoughts. It doesn't matter that he is here in London, because the collective subconscious he wanders through on his inner journeys belongs to his native land and to his native tongue. It is hard to say if it's a conscious choice he made in the past, or whether bit by bit he withdrew from day-to-day interactions in the world because of a trauma or a series of traumas. Or maybe a lasting disappointment at what the world has to offer has changed everything. His physical presence in his flat is very light, as if he isn't really living here, as if his real home is a far more wondrous, luminous, and fluid point outside time and space.

In his presence it's easy to sense peace, acceptance and serenity. In many ways he isn't really living here, but only sheltering his physical body from the elements, from the long rainy night that surprised us all last week with its relentlessness, and from rainy nights to come. His true home, his true being, is a long way from here. Through the years he has fanned the spark of gnosis inside him into a wondrously living flame.

I mention Elijah's depression in the wilderness, when he shelters under a juniper tree and prays for death to take him. And I speak of John of the Cross's night of the soul, a test of faith, a journey of change. What if what we know as depression is an awakening, an invitation to take on a number of challenges in the world that we are profoundly resistant to? What if depression is as much a spiritual problem as anything else? Solomon is alert and listening fully when I talk of such things. I am speaking the words he loves to hear and he would sit there all day listening sympathetically. In the world of spirit, he is on a different level. In a certain sense he is not really present in the world, and it is as if he has simply outgrown it.

Coming across people like Solomon, the holy fool comes to mind, the archetype from Russian folklore known as *yurodivy*. Often ridiculed and on the outside of society, such archetypes still speak of truths others can't see, and like Elijah they come upon us as lone strangers living by a brook and fed by ravens. When he wrestled a stranger at Penuel, Jacob found God (Genesis 32), and in welcoming strangers Abraham found out he was to be a father (Genesis 18). Although the ancient tradition of welcoming strangers, because they might be angels in disguise or bringers of important news, has lessened in these days of stranger danger, there is still a spiritual lesson attached to such meetings.

I once saw a registered state nurse chasing what looked like a young homeless man away from the corridor of a public hospital.

Such cruelty seemed to come from nowhere. The man was poorly dressed and looked like he hadn't eaten a decent meal in quite a while. He had been soaked by the rain and was harmlessly drying his rain-drenched jacket on a radiator in an empty corridor that led nowhere. Who knows where he slept the night before, when he last ate, or where he would sleep that night? There was no harm in allowing him to stay there and warm up on a cold wet day and dry his jacket on an unused radiator. Weakened by life and scared of an authority figure in a nurse's uniform who threatened him with security, he took his wet jacket and quickly left without a word.

I looked at the nurse as she walked past: defiance and cruelty were in her eyes. There was no need to do something like that. It wasn't her role to show such contempt and cruelty to someone who was simply trying to stay alive. She had clearly not given much thought to the possible bad luck that might result from showing such unkindness to strangers on a cold wet day.

> Do not neglect to show kindness to strangers; for in this way, some, without knowing it, have angels as their guests. (Hebrews 13:2)

I took note of her name-badge as she passed as I had a mind to report her. I was so caught up with mental health work at the time, I didn't get around to doing it, and I wasn't sure if I should have done so anyway. I doubt it would have made much difference to anyone. But her name stayed with me as a reminder of the casual cruelty running in myriad patterns through so much of life. If she could do that to a man who looked half-scared to death and soaked to the skin on such a day, what else could she do?

A few months later I overheard a couple of mental health nurses taking about a nurse who had just dropped dead in the prime of life. She was from the same hospital they worked in, the same hospital where I had seen that act of cruelty. I asked her name, and it was the same as the nurse who had chased the frightened and sopping-wet stranger away from a radiator in a public hospital. I didn't look into it beyond that. It was probably her: I couldn't say for sure. Her sudden death was probably unconnected to her cruelty to a stranger on that wet day. Or maybe it wasn't. There was something chilling about her as far as I can remember, as if she had already died a spiritual death, or some important part of her had.

Solomon tells me how once he walked from Asmara into the desert without food, water, or shelter. He walked under the sun for days without any reason to do so. But somehow he survived and fell by a roadside and sat there for hours until a passing truck picked him up. When he speaks about his time in the desert, his eyes light up. By retelling his experiences and reconnecting emotionally with them, he touches a higher spiritual energy. His eyes become lightships, which shoot out what could be called divine light. Why should he join us psychic serfs in a dead-spirited world with our feet of clay? Having travelled in the kingdom of his own mind, is there anywhere of wonder and joy he has got easier access to by means of his own human gifts? He has wandered red-dust deserts under a blistering African sun.

He has walked without anything to eat or drink, until he was walking on spirit itself. Why barter the nobility of his inner life for the present-day parallel of a pauper-lunatic's confinement? Happy pills aside, what can a Western shaman of the mind offer Solomon? At times in our conversation his eyes are glazed as if it's not me he's seeing but rather shaytans and the eddies of red dust that desert tribesmen once chased with sabres, to kill the demon in the eye of the storm. I can't help thinking of things I have read about the spirits of mountains, forests, and rivers. If it is true that the spirits of nature enter the spirit of humankind, then the deserts west of Asmara have changed Solomon's spirit with the result that their power is here at this strange and restless crossroads. The dark enigma of his eyes is fashioned from the sun's energy. Inflections in his soft utterances are the depths of time itself. At least here he is free from tyrants and the brutality of police and militias. He traverses the metropolis with his gaze on the ground ahead much like he would have done in his desert forays.

He tolerates us much like a buffalo at a waterhole tolerates flies buzzing about its ears. People like us are employed to try and coax him into the world we are part of. If we are successful he can live like all the other modern-day pauper-lunatics, like the rest of us who are never so very far away from poverty or stress-related meltdown or medical catastrophe. The perversity of all this defies everyday logic. Here's this mystic, this gentle soul who shrugs off hardships most of us could hardly endure at all, and who is perpetually kind in word and deed.

In a saner scenario we would be his students, hanging on to the few words he speaks, and allowing the silences between his words and the silence in his eyes to enter our hearts. In another time or another corner of the globe we would listen closely to all he has to say. We would listen in the hope of hearing about a similar route to an inner world of enlightened peace. But here in this time and in this place he is just another mental health outpatient farmed out to a mental health charity. We try to coax his thoughts towards a societal reality, urging him to be more like us. We are so starved of mystics that when one shows up in front of us, we cannot recognise him for who he is.

We talk about the desert, about how the sun guides the mind into fantastical vistas after only a matter of hours. And how the senses are reawakened and reset so that the simplest touch, taste or sight is exhilarating, and how the evening and the night invite mischievous spirits. On more than one occasion, hyenas passed so close to where he rested that he could smell the sour odour of their breath and the stench of their fur. Like the lions when faced with Daniel, the hyenas were also passive as they passed the slumbering Solomon. The truer lessons of earlier times unfold for him on his daily ten- or sometimes twenty-mile walks through London and its suburbs.

Wisdom is unfolding in him as his spirit grows to take in more fully the truths of his desert rambles. I can't see how anything I might say or do could help him to work out what he needs to work out. In his case the categorisation of mental illness is a metaphor for a spiritual awakening, which is impressive enough to take years to manifest fully. I am blessed to see this happening, this unfolding of a human narrative which is experimental only in our interpretations. It is universal and as old as humankind itself. Meanwhile news from the psychiatry labs is unsurprisingly fixated on the modifications of chemical processes in the body. In a recent article in a leading newspaper a King's College psychiatrist is quoted saying that we are between five and ten years away from a blood test that will measure levels of inflammation in depressed persons. This latest exciting moment in popular psychiatry champions drugs which are not only important to neurology, but to inflammation too. The journalist gets carried away towards the end of the article as he proclaims we are five years away from a cure for depression. The article then refers to a global epidemic of depression.

We have heard it before, the magical pills shaken from the conjure-bag of the Western shaman. We have heard the announcement reassigning our suffering as something that can be readjusted by manipulating our neurological chemicals. Again, the propaganda reasserts the primary idea of mental disorder as centred in the brain, when we know it is much more multifaceted, and often a great deal simpler. Mostly it's about who we are as people and the diminishment of human worth, to values fixed to indifferent economic statistics and a professed status in the game of life. It's about what we have lost and the future losses to come, about unheard voices and silent screams piercing disconnections between generations. The real disease is the reductive materialist mindset, destructive technology, and hyper-consumerism that we have sleepwalked into and the cultural and ecological vandalism it leaves in the wake of its self-identified progress. The cure for the disease is to sweeten the pill, to medicate, coerce or zombify the patient or the neurotic into compliance. The journalist is right in one sense, because there is a global epidemic of depression. It has been partially caused by an ideology of radical hyper-consumerism and by the shortcomings of our most empowered hierarchies. Only in mythology, religious codes, archetypes, mysticism, folklore, and an understanding of the dead and our relationship to them, can we hope to discover who and what we really are. A faith in the future can't help us with this.

There is real satisfaction in spending time with Solomon. Somehow against the odds he has escaped the psychic tyranny pressing on all our souls. He is the medieval fool from the tarot deck who breaks free from the tyrant's gaze by slipping past everyday logic. By remaining polite and quiet, he has escaped the fuller gaze of the psychiatrists and they have written him off as an imbecile with uninteresting underlying mental health symptoms. They prescribe antidepressants which he mostly doesn't take. He is not important enough to be supervised by a community psychiatric nurse or an NHS recovery worker. So they have passed him down the line to us lowly mental health charity support workers. Contrary to appearances, he is freer than most of the wage-slaves involved in his initial hospitalisation and subsequent care.

Whatever he witnessed in the deserts west of Asmara it stays with him to this day. His aura is still tinged with the colours of red-dust deserts, and his eyes have seen truths we spend so much of our lives avoiding. He is a messenger from another place, and he communicates volumes with his very presence. Little wonder they have written him off as a madman for in the eyes of the orthodoxy only a madman could be so fulfilled while being a pauper.

Marcia

Another location is needed for the work that is to come. London is simply too congested. There is far too much light pollution, and not enough space and privacy. It's spiritually congested too. It's possible to walk through most streets and sense the presence of spirits who have not gone far after death, known as earthbound spirits. On one street on my way from work in the evenings their presence is very strong. If there was time to stop and concentrate on the auras in the street, it would not take much effort to understand why those spirits have not gone far. It might even be possible to see them in one shape or other. But who has that sort of free time?

After visiting the site of the old Cane Hill Asylum, it's easier to sense the negative spiritual energy in parts of London. Spiritually there are many unresolved issues here. If anyone here is planning a conjuration involving earthbound spirits or entities from the Astral Plane, this then is the right place to reopen the magical records of the experimentalists, who were fierce in their courage and intellect. Without rituals outside state-controlled monotheism or state-influenced literalism, and without community cohesion, a connection to nature, and a mental health system which takes into view the fuller dimensions of the human spirit, then naturally the beginning of the search for gnosis is yet further obscured.

Not unsurprisingly, crime rates shoot up and children stab each other in the streets and grown-ups jump to their deaths in front of trains. What other outcomes can be expected?

In the middle of the working week there is a full moon on a clear night. Only a few generations ago a legacy of Anglo-Saxon-Celtic worship could still be found in the villages and hamlets of the shires. To see the first moon through glass, even the glass of spectacles, was bad luck. The manuscripts of the Anglo-Saxon charms held at the British Museum are keepers of old cures. "When the moon is waning tie glove-wort with red thread around the neck of the lunatic." Not so long ago this natural environment was a mysterious and magical backdrop to our lives. Now we see the moon, and on some nights perhaps remember a line or two of poetry, or we see conspiracy, or nothing at all.

I am on my way to see Marcia. She has had several hospital admissions for bulimia, self-harm, and slashing her wrists in a hot bath. I have only met her once before and was touched by her fragility and impressed by her willingness to keep going. She is just about hanging on. That's the thought I have after meeting her. And whatever she is hanging on to is not very secure either. The phone is busy for almost the entire journey: texts, missed calls, voice messages, and brief conversations with both mental health outpatients and workers from other agencies. There's anger in some of what's said, or maybe a kind of subverted rage or raw frustration. It's not blatant but rather unstated, at least in words.

People are bouncing around their frustrations here and there, workers from alcohol services and a social worker who—in theory at least—had responsibility for coordinating Tina's care-plan. They are not wilfully blaming anyone, but frustration is finding a home in their emotions. They come across needing to blame someone for Tina's death. It happens. The system is unsuited to solving the problems it is given to solve. Maybe such a system can never be found or pieced together using what we have. Maybe it's mostly an illusion, a conjuring trick dressed up in the gladrags of humanist evolution. It grinds on like an old clapped-out tractor up a mucky hill. And then when someone dies or kills someone or has a part in a crime or incident involving the police where answers are needed, the blame game goes into overdrive.

Often it's a random scapegoat as it is physically impossible to get through all the tasks, responsibilities and record-keeping duties in the allocated time. So everyone is potentially a scapegoat. Someone will take the implied blame for Tina's death, depending on what level of fuss the friends and family kick up. But usually the implications of blame are hardly noticeable. There might be a friendly-sounding neutral question or two asked by a line-manager during monthly supervision. How much time exactly did you spend with Tina? Were you happy with the liaison between the various agencies involved in her care? Is there anything you might have done differently?

Managers in social care, mental health charities, and the NHS have carved out golden careers from the simple task of pushing blame onto others. They do this while at the same time fabricating an impression that the tragedy in question was bound to happen and the institution as a whole is blameless. When anything serious happens, or when nothing at all is happening, there is always a niggling fear of a call from a manager. The first question they then ask is the beginning of the scapegoating ordeal. Usually it blows over quickly and there is little damage done other than to the feelings of the random scapegoat. It can be sensed in the messages questioning Tina's death, sensed on the way to see Marcia: the irrepressible urge to blame someone.

I scrape a bit of money together and buy an old Ford Focus. With such a workhorse to hand, getting around to see people is much easier. The hassle of waiting for buses is replaced by the hassle of finding somewhere to park. I pull into a sideroad to read through Marcia's referral paperwork. I emailed her referral worker but haven't heard back from him yet. This is normal, the work carried through at a chaotic pace with never enough time to do justice to any of the crucial stages of the referral process and the initial assessments. Everyone is too busy to spend anything but the bare minimum of time on every task. Not to be busy is inexcusable.

Marcia had a breakdown. She went through a bad year where several events in her life tipped everything upside down. Her mother died. Her long-term boyfriend ran away with someone else. She was arrested and charged with drunk-driving. She began to lose her ability to concentrate. She had trouble meeting her monthly targets at work. She began crying in public. One more upset could send her somewhere she would find it very hard to come back from.

I am early so I park and kill time with a detour through an old shopping mall and into one of London's parks beneath a quaint railway arch that belongs to another time. I pass tennis courts where people are larking about with rackets, laughing when they whack a serve into the nets. Others walk prim little house-dogs and nervous rescue-dogs. and a woman in a curious headscarf is tossing crumbs to grateful pigeons. In seconds the green spaces work on the inner avenues of my mind. This corner of the world is not such an urgent or crowded place to be. And then on past bowling greens, flowerbeds and a duck-pond, which allow nature to filter into my unconscious thoughts and my very being. There is an urge to keep walking, to traverse London through its parks and then to slog on past the boundary of the M25 and on further to the sea.

I allow the fantasy to fill my mind for a circuit of the duck-pond and then I check my watch. There is time to sit on a park bench for a little while before making my way to where Marcia lives. Any possible trek into the country inspired by Solomon's wanderings in the red-dust deserts west of Asmara will have to wait for another day. On the bench by the pond I mull over the routes leading here to this very moment. I try to rationalise the impulse to go to such lengths to find answers to the psychic agony at the core of what's troubling the outpatients in our care. I ask myself, is it really my concern? The system, with all its resources and experts, can't or won't prevent people from drinking themselves to death. Why do I think I can offer anything better than the desultory efforts of statutory systems of care and rehabilitation, and so many disposable workers who were here before me. There is no hope of finding resources with which to build an independent structure of support. Is any of this really my problem? Is there any kind of workable structure for healing here?

For a while, as I quietly watch the ducks, I am troubled by the self-destructiveness that so often drives contemporary addictions. It often feels like someone somewhere taps the genetic code of self-destruction into the addict's DNA. Then the biological fall into total meltdown and annihilation is set in motion. Six of my vulnerable adults are drugging and drinking themselves to death. Others are lost to mental illness, despair, and the everyday pain of consciousness. The only way to survive it emotionally is to step back from them, to build stronger boundaries, and to keep a professional distance. To step too close to the abyss of addiction is dangerous. When we see it objectively, we see the nature of death without resurrection. We wait in the shadow of a lifeforce chained heavily to the wheel of suffering. There is a cascade of doubt at the very core of this day. There's a weariness too, an entropy in dark grey that is not in any hurry to pass.

I know I need to connect with the energy flows in my body through breathing exercises, to clear my mind of the dirge of negativity lodging there rent-free. I remember an arcane method I had read about for reviving the mind and body and, in the relative peace by the duck-pond, there is privacy enough to use it. But there is a strangeness bellying into the very centre of these moments. I am too tired to use my mind to shake off the fatigue, helpless in the face of addictions which are raging in the lives of the vulnerable adults in my care. For now, I am helpless. The malignance of addictions mutates into a physical manifestation. They transmute the personality of the afflicted over a given span of time. It's passed on through the epigenetics, scientists say, or something of that nature as they ponder the missing heritability problem.

There is a broader truth in their words. The sins of the father that are visited on the son. We mention epigenetic possibilities and Faraday's field theory, while other cultures mention ancestors. The percentages are startling when alcoholism is a factor on both or even just one side of the family. There's no argument. The only thing I might add is that demons or spirits not at peace can live in families too. And they can jump through the genes like other afflictions and predispositions. Ancestors angered, genes and energy fields unfavourable. The only thing I can say for sure is that, to take an active role against addictions, we must be strong, rested, and supported by others just as committed to work for the same results. All those conditions are now absent and my eyes are closing.

There's a shout from nearby and my eyes shoot open. I must have dozed off for a minute or so. Senses quickly tune into a series of further shouts. I relax as there is nothing to worry about, just kids kicking a ball on the grass on the other side of the duck-pond. Seconds later I am on my feet and hurrying back the way I came, towards the street where Marcia lives. I am tired enough to literally sleep for a week, but such things hardly matter. Here there is no sleep or rest, not here in this sea of strange turbulence. By the time I get to the railway-arch exit of the park I am awake enough to get on with what remains of the working day, to crack on with what needs to be done, and then hopefully head for home without any disastrous loss of energy.

I am almost out the park entrance when Kenny rings. I take the call hoping he hasn't lapsed into one of his spirals of doom or isn't sitting at home getting ready to set fire to his flat again. But straightaway I can tell by his voice he is in a good space. He's got news for me he says, big news. He's leaving London. He has had enough and mentions a town far away in the shires. His brother has a caravan out the back of a small cottage he inherited from his grandparents and has offered it to Kenny rent-free. And he is not under any probation service conditions or restrictions from the authorities. Technically nobody can prevent him from leaving.

But the mental health workers supervising his outpatient care are doing all they can to talk him into not going. It is what he expected them to do, to try and prevent him from living in the countryside far away from the chaos of London. It fits in with his wider theory of how the system is trying to kill him by keeping him in his flat, where he's convinced he'll be dead inside a year or two:

> They're just evil bastards mate, trying to kill people like me off, they are. They're doing all they can to stop me from going to live with my brother, but they can sod off. I'm going. If I stay here another year, they'll carry me out of that flat in a box, and it's exactly what they want. But I've had enough, I'm going.

I almost punch the air and shout down the phone in solidarity. At last Kenny is making decisions about his life independent of what psychiatrists, social workers, doctors, and mental health workers are instructing him to do. He wants to know if we can do another ritual of burning negative links to the past before he leaves London forever. He thinks the earlier ritual helped him a lot and he has one particular bad memory he'd like to focus on. I say no problem, I'd be happy to help. It would give us a chance to meet up for the last time and say our goodbyes before this new stage in his life. There is a Native American tribe who greet each other with two short questions: "What are your words of death?" and, "What are your words of life?" What he says over the phone are words of life, momentous words rescuing him from a snare he is certain will kill him. This time I am with him one hundred percent.

He tended to be ignored or underestimated by those he encountered, but his thought-life could be startlingly insightful. He admitted his bleak outlook on life and lucid moments on LSD and other drugs had confirmed the worse. In a universe that counts in billions of years, an average human lifespan or even the lifespan of an entire civilisation is short and meaningless. What do the great pyramids of Giza or the other wonders of the world mean in a universe of such terrifying indifference and such fearful allusion? He has pondered our overall encompassment and concluded that, in light of the age of the universe and the mysteries of its creation and design, life is at the end of the day meaningless and terrifying. What can a psychiatrist say to shift such a worldview? Based on reductive logic, and on the wisdom of analytical thinkers weaned all their lives on hard science, life is of course meaningless. Only when he touched the divine spark within through the *Hymn to the Sun* and a simple ritual did the meaningless of an increasingly nihilistic and narcissistic culture shift slightly. Hopefully we will have more conversations and more time to look at other routes to meaning and to gnosis.

On the street where Marcia lives, the weather is just as crazy as ever, or perhaps even crazier. Often in London we get four seasons in one day, or sometimes in one hour. The week before, I got talking to the lady in the corner-shop and she mentioned one recent morning when it was raining out the back of her house while the sun was shining out the front. It scared her as she had never seen anything like it in her native country. She sensed it meant something important but didn't know what. Maybe our weather experts need to get in touch with those Inuit elders to ask them about how the earth has strayed off its axis, and what it really means.

The apparatus of psychiatric assessment and care serves the gods of materialist vested interest as an overriding priority and are fully signed up to the ignorance of the materialist world as created by an ignorant creator. The reduction of our humanity feeds a wave of addictions and mental disorders. We are gods in our innermost parts, atoms of Gottfried de Purucker's spiritual sun. But, in the eyes of the psychiatric structures of assessment, we are too often guinea pigs or useful numbers for the psychopharmacology industry.

Our true worth is in our capacity to consume rather than in our natural human identity and potential. We are alienated from our environment and from assimilation with the cosmos. Existential psychology in its broader application falls short out here in these fields of suffering. As much as human problems need human remedies, extra-mundane problems need extra-mundane remedies. We are asked to live in a world without wonder.

Again and again our unimaginative, secular answers to the complex inferences of mental disorder leave us perplexed and dissatisfied. The respected and rational inquiries by Bergson and Jung regarding the existence of consciousness outside mental states are ignored by psychiatrists. From such inquiries it is too short a jump to the likelihood of a source of consciousness not centred in the human mind. And if such a consciousness can exist, then it can credibly communicate with the mentally disordered patient.

Such an idea can never be prioritised when we are signed up to a very different cultural and ecological pathway. Demons have settled in the thoughts of the psychopharmacology mandarins and their fellow travellers in the grander psychiatric project. They cannot be expunged for the lie is universal. Demons don't exist. Most of us can accept that mental disorder is about many things: a lack of love or understanding, a lack of initiation into manhood, or an absence of ritual. Or exclusion from secular rituals because of a lack of family support or because of socio-economic circumstances. Or genetic predisposition, low IQ, life-trauma, or even the spiritual and psychic pitfalls our culture once had an awareness of, but not anymore. Rarely is it simply about the regulation of certain chemicals in our brains. Neither is it necessarily always connected with the individual's failure to fit in with roles and tasks they find intolerable. The masquerade continues.

Marcia is not answering her doorbell. I hang around for a minute or two and try again but there's still no answer. I make a few phone-calls and, after the familiar problems with communications between the agencies involved in mental health and the usual confusion, I find out that she has been readmitted to the local psychiatric hospital.

I am happy for her in a way. It's where I sensed she really wanted to be. On the trains and buses, and in the shops and queues of the metropolis, the noise from other people's earphones and from public speakers and traffic is increasing. The general hubbub adds up to something like the white noise still used to torture political prisoners in parts of the world. I think about Marcia, suffering such noise day in and day out, as she wrestles with the traumas in her life. What the biomedical model of psychiatric assessment classifies as her mental disorder makes a lot more sense. It's testimony to her courage in making it this far. Don't we all, or most of us, endure the white noise of modernity without cracking or running to nature and never returning. Maybe there are Guardian Angels or Astral Bodies out there, or the twenty-four paternal and maternal angels of *The Book of Baruch* or an external agency urging us on unaided by ideas relating to biological evolution. Surely somebody or something must be looking out for us.

Yesterday there were several articles in the mainstream print media covering the mental health crisis:

> Man Jumped to Death after Hospital Refused to Admit Him

And

> Mental Health Mistakes: Hundreds of Deaths in Custody are Preventable

The articles portray NHS mental health staff as being overwhelmed by clinical duties and sketch a series of shortcomings and too-often-puny answers from mental health officials around severe mental disorder. The cases are increasing and are there in the media for us to study every single day if we feel so inclined. Suicides, murders, assaults. Or a combined explosion of rage where innocents are butchered by a family member who goes on to commit suicide. The news from so many crossroads confirms a crisis in mental health.

There are not enough resources in the present system, and the method of assessment and care is flawed anyway. No matter how many suicides and murders are marked down to mental disorder and the failings of the present assessment and hospital admission process, the psychiatrists still don't believe that a review of their overall ethos is needed. Stories in the media stack up one after the other and the first-hand accounts from NHS workers on the ground are buried in dry reports on suicides and psychiatric killings. Many other crimes and suicides are reported without reference to mental health causal factors, when we know that they are involved.

Ongoing judicial reviews, public inquiries, and various committees make heroic efforts at uncovering what the problem is and how it can be improved. But nothing of importance ever happens. Nothing changes and nothing is resolved. More mental health wards are closed. The tide of mental health disorder washes over a volume of rhetoric from those on the sidelines as if it doesn't really exist. The will just isn't there to investigate the root cause of what is termed mental disorder.

An illusion of post-Christian, humanist progress overrides the more pressing questions being asked at the more harried pace of the modern crossroads. Cultural identity and fraternity, familial and community support, the mysteries of our past, spiritual solemnity and ritual, respect for ancestors, and a spiritual relationship with nature are lost to the illusions of the age. These appalling losses are accepted as the cost of progress. People may feel they are gaining something from the spiritual and cultural vandalism at the heart of modernity. But where does it really take us?

Surely none of us are served by cultural nihilism. Healers of earlier times asked simple questions of those with symptoms of depression. When did you stop singing? When did you stop dancing? When did you cease to be enchanted by stories? When did you stop sensing the mystery of the universe in silence? Holistic healing is an art of intonation and vibration of divine names as much as invoking spiritual energy. Now the modern shaman shakes yet more pills from his or her conjure-bag and tells us the good news that it's really all about the chemical imbalance in our brains. Medicated in this way and most likely sickened by side-effects and with the chemicals in our brains distorted, we struggle on in a world stripped of spiritual and esoteric meaning. The increase in psychic suffering we see all around us and the epidemic of depression referenced earlier are more steps on the road to cultural and spiritual impoverishment. With the present increase in the rates of diagnosis, soon everyone will be afflicted or will know somebody afflicted by one sub-category or other of what we generally understand as mental disorder.

Our cultural impoverishment hit home a short time ago when I showed up for the funeral of a former mental health patient who died in a flat which he did not want to live in. He was cremated in a large London cemetery. Four other mourners were present. Several others were expected to show up but for whatever reason they didn't. The deceased's last wish was for the pop song *Losing My Religion* to be played at the crematorium. A non-conformist minister wearing only a small silver cross pinned to her lapel as a badge of office showed up late. While the track was playing, I glanced at the minister as she had closed her eyes and must have been wondering what she was doing there.

There were few flowers, no tears, and not much ceremony. The minister shook everyone's hands and did all she could to lift the tearless assembly into the semblance of a gathering for the departed. Overall it was miserable because the rites of departing life were not honoured. The decision to play a song like that dishonoured the occasion. After all it was the final ceremony in the life of a human being. When I spoke about how difficult I found the funeral to a friend she said she had read somewhere that *Losing My Religion* is one of the more popular songs played at funerals.

Alongside ritual-free funerals is the increase in what's known as direct cremations. In this case there is no ceremony at all, no attendance by family and friends, and no rituals. The next of kin who choose direct cremations point out that in an age of austerity such cremations cost a third of general cremations.

At this crossroads we have mostly lost the habit of listening to elders, shamans, and the whisperings of nature, believing that we have all we need in the few cubic centimetres inside our skulls, where we are told our consciousness begins and ends. This is probably okay when things are going tolerably well. But on a morning of crisis the absence of so many important cultural norms and assurances is often the difference between coping and not coping. The NHS and its privatised proxies have become as close to a national religion as anything else we have. In the absence of so many folk and arcane reassurances, a multitude of GPs and psychiatrists are now reduced versions of our confessors, our healers, our spiritual guides and our fetish-priests.

More all-inclusive and human-centred criteria for mental health assessment are needed, even if they are at odds with a deeply strange psychiatric structure obsessed with medication and conformity. We have a duty to our own survival to widen the parameters of discourse and insist that the human narrative in mental disorder supersedes the psychopharmacological hegemony and profit principle. There must be a human counterbalance to normative and reductive mechanisms, and to the levels of careerism in the mental health hierarchies. And, as part of these new parameters, it makes great sense to include the likelihood of intelligence independent of human minds as a factor in mental disorder. Isn't it wiser to think about a universally accepted correlation between mental disorder and earthbound spirits, astral shells, and energies from the Astral Plane? Isn't it just and fair to keep an open mind on the healing legacy of gnosis? Just because our models of mental health interventions are bleakly atheistic in outlook does not in itself rule out spiritual principles or silence the voices of mental health patients who may be seen as demonised.

Another therapy underused by the Western shaman, or doctors and psychiatrists if you prefer, is meditation. Based on ongoing research with DBT clients and the word of many who meditate regularly, it would be a helpful move to promote meditation for those suffering from stress and depression. With its excellent recorded outcomes we would be careless not to. When psychiatrists lead their patients and staff in short meditation or mindfulness sessions, we will know something very important has shifted.

Reflecting on Proclus's *Hymn to the Sun* and the ritual of fire in Kenny's kitchen sink is also helpful. Stepping outside hierarchical power dynamics, and relating primarily from where we find ourselves as people who are disconnected from our cultural roots, can make more sense of the misery and abuse someone in Kenny's situation associates with the system and its dreary tentacles. I made myself vulnerable by mentioning the arcane. He trusted me more because of it. Disassociating myself from state power, I began to communicate with Kenny, which meant that he listened to what I had to say.

Both Kenny and Big Tam from pre-regeneration Kings Cross were really searching for a way out of a dependency on a system they despised. Our mental health charity was a small part in the revelation whereby they began to understand that there is more in the world than we are led to believe. There is a spark of divine truth inside all of us, whether we wish to deny it or not. And anyhow, we never really know the effects we have in the lives of others. With Nicos and Solomon it is impossible to see them as independent from the spiritual traditions which transformed their inner lives. They are a kind of mendicant, their suffering and alienation an emblem of a deeper, collective malaise. They are categorised as mentally disordered, because their spiritual aspirations are not defined by the time we live in and by society's expectations at this moment.

Given how things stand at present, they will never be accepted for their extraordinary sensitivity, but tolerated instead as long as they are docile and keep taking their meds. Gareth survives through art, and lives through art. Although the word is that he is not doing well lately and will probably need a hospital bed again soon, he finds meaning in translating ideas and images in his mind through his art pencils and computer tools. Art saves him from the worse outcomes of his condition.

Why our paths crossed I am not exactly sure. In the quietest recess of my heart, I have regularly asked myself the same query, questioned every facet of my life in caring for vulnerable adults and ransacked my consciousness for answers. I don't really know why I have given so much of my life to the project of caring for casualties of modernity at this curious crossroads of life. As one of our modern magi once said, when we are in the place we are meant to be, then we have the inertia of the universe to assist us. The more I think it over the more it makes sense. Looking for gnosis in others helps to locate my own source of gnosis.

The best examples of London-based African visionaries and healers make possible a transition for the individual in psychic crisis, in certain cases to the humble role of healer. Even if we are mediocre healers, it matters little, since the planet and its peoples need as many healers as they can get.

It was too late for Tina even before we met. I only hope her partner and her sister manage to arrange a funeral with grief, sacred words, and ritual. It's the least she deserves. Through the grapevine the word is that her case is not straightforward. Those closest to her cannot afford to bury her. They are too short on funds to raise the cost of a funeral at today's prices. They are hoping the council can help. Throughout London the bodies of the poor are freeze-stored in the public morgues. The councils do not want the expense of burying them, so they store them, waiting for the families and loved ones to come up with the burial fees. They will wait for months if necessary. With the very poor cases, they will eventually relent and accept that nobody is going to offer to cover the funeral costs. Then the council will confer the present-day version of the pauper's funeral. And the family members who haven't coughed up won't be invited. It is hard to picture the scene of Tina stored away as a frozen cadaver in a public morgue while those closest to her scramble about for the funds to bury her. It's the final indignation in a line of indignations going back in time.

Tristan the friendly psychiatrist finally caught up with Eddie. After a few fractious conversations, it was decided that Eddie should be held for assessment under the Mental Health Act in a local psychiatric ward. Unfortunately, I was present for most of the drama, and Eddie blamed me personally for his worst possible nightmare. Sadly, one gets sucked into such torments. But presently we must leave all this to one side. There is only a given span of time for these meditations. We must always remember to sing, dance, and be enchanted by stories. We are stars after all in our innermost parts. The *Round Dance of the Cross* is meant to be danced. And there is still much living and healing ahead.

There is hope from optimistic voices which are countering the nihilism of the materialist prejudice of our times in many ways. Atheist philosophers are now rallying many spiritually bereft followers to both online and actual hubs of pseudo-spirituality. Analysing results of positive psychology research, atheist philosophers and public intellectuals realise that there are beneficial results from religious and spiritual practice. Meditation, chanting or singing with others, pilgrimages, gratitude and other activities, and attitudes associated with religious and spiritual devotion are actually good for us. Atheists are missing out on these psychological and health benefits and are adapting religious and spiritual codes into an atheist framework. The penny is dropping. We cannot live like this for much longer.

In these pages we have touched on aspects of the lives and care of people struggling at the very bottom rung of the social ladder. Many of them are just about hanging in there. Holistic approaches that keep in mind our fundamental humanity and need for transcendence have real import. A sludge of negative, atheistic, and pessimistic beliefs are shaming and coercing populations into a radically materialist mentality that reduces human beings to a lesser version of what we could be. It is a miserabilist's cipher that sees only atoms and neutrons instead of the mystery and magic of the cosmos, its potentiality, and our place in it.

It all seems futile anyway. As the respected neuropsychiatrist and near-death researcher Peter Fenwick points out, when pronounced atheists are dying, they realise they have been wrong all along. Something very different begins to happen, a sequence of events totally opposed to the stark nihilism they have lived their lives by. Atheism falls away and they look on in astonishment at the unfolding of a reality of awesome dimensions. From the baseline of our humanity, we owe more to the vulnerable among us, to the casualties of relentless competitiveness and pathetic egoism dressed up as virtue or pragmatism. It is probably time for the Western mind to reconnect with its humanity and see beyond the lab technician's microscope and the financial analyst's projections of growth for the coming quarter.

We will surely learn more about how we are meant to respond to addictions in our healing role. If we are successful, lives can be saved. One life would be enough. Knowledge from these other realms must be respected and held in confidence. It is not research or knowledge that can be published in a psychology paper or in the newsletter of a mental health charity. The search for answers goes on, often in directions ignored by our social care and psychiatric hierarchies. The cosmic light of the divine shines within all of us and the quest for meaning and love goes on. In the mornings, especially when the sun is in view, the quest is as real and as authentic as a human heartbeat. Our masquerade becomes a celebration of life itself and of the mysteries that sustain life.

POSTSCRIPT

I bumped into Tina's partner on the high street, but he couldn't talk for long as he was running late for the pub. I said I was really sorry we couldn't do more to save her. He shrugged and said the council eventually got around to cremating her and he scattered her ashes in her favourite park. I suggested a commemoration service in the park where her ashes were scattered, as the location must have meant something to her. Her partner said it was a nice idea but looked preoccupied and said he really had to go.

We chose All Soul's Day to commemorate the life of Tina. I invited her partner but he didn't show up. I invited several voluntary sector workers who had supported her in one capacity or other but they either didn't get back to me or were vague in their answers. They didn't show up either. I asked two friends who had never known her to come with me and the three of us went to the park she loved in her lifetime. The park was close to where she lived and was easy enough to get to.

We brought flowers and placed them on a timber bench in a quiet corner of the park. We stood quietly together and I spoke a little about her life and struggles. I pronounced her full name clearly and described her character and kind nature. I then opened a notebook and read Margaret Mead's poem *Remember Me*:

> To the living, I am gone,
> To the sorrowful, I will never return,
> To the angry, I was cheated,
> But to the happy, I am at peace,
> And to the faithful, I have never left.
> I cannot speak, but I can listen.
> I cannot be seen, but I can be heard.
> So as you stand upon a shore gazing at a beautiful sea,
> As you look upon a flower and admire its simplicity,
>   remember me.
> Remember me in your heart:
> Your thoughts, and your memories,
> Of the times we loved,
> The times we cried,
> The times we fought,
> The times we laughed.
> For if you always think of me, I will never have gone.

I closed my notebook and put it back in my pocket. The friend standing next to me raised her head a little and murmured something I didn't catch. We stood together in silence for some moments and from our hearts radiated love to the departed spirit of a friend. A raven landed on the grass nearby and looked at us curiously. Squirrels from a nearby oak seemed to notice us too. We were united for some moments with nature and with the spirits of nature. It was a meaningful sequence of moments. We placed the flowers we had brought more centrally on the bench and turned in the direction of the park's exit gate. We had remembered Tina and prayed for her soul. It was now time for us to go on with our lives in the world of the living.

www.ingramcontent.com/pod-product-compliance
Ingram Content Group UK Ltd.
Pitfield, Milton Keynes, MK11 3LW, UK
UKHW021015120926
8556IPUK00040B/1160

9 781801 522151